God and Man in African Religion

A case study of the Igbo of Nigeria

Dr Emefie Ikenga Metuh

Geoffrey Chapman
London

Geoffrey Chapman book published by
Cassell Ltd, 35 Red Lion Square, London WC1R 4SG
and at Sydney, Auckland, Toronto
an affiliate of Macmillan Publishing Co Inc, New York

First published 1981
British Library Cataloguing in Publication Data
Metuh, Emefie Ikenga
  God and man in African religion
  1. Ibo tribe – Religion and mythology
  I. Title
  299'.683   DT515
ISBN 0 225 66279 5

Typeset by Inforum Ltd, Portsmouth
Printed and bound in Great Britain at
The Camelot Press Ltd, Southampton

In memory of my late Dad
Chief Sir Augustine Ikenga Metuh
The Ochiagha of Nnewi-Otolo
who inspired me to
undertake this
study

Contents

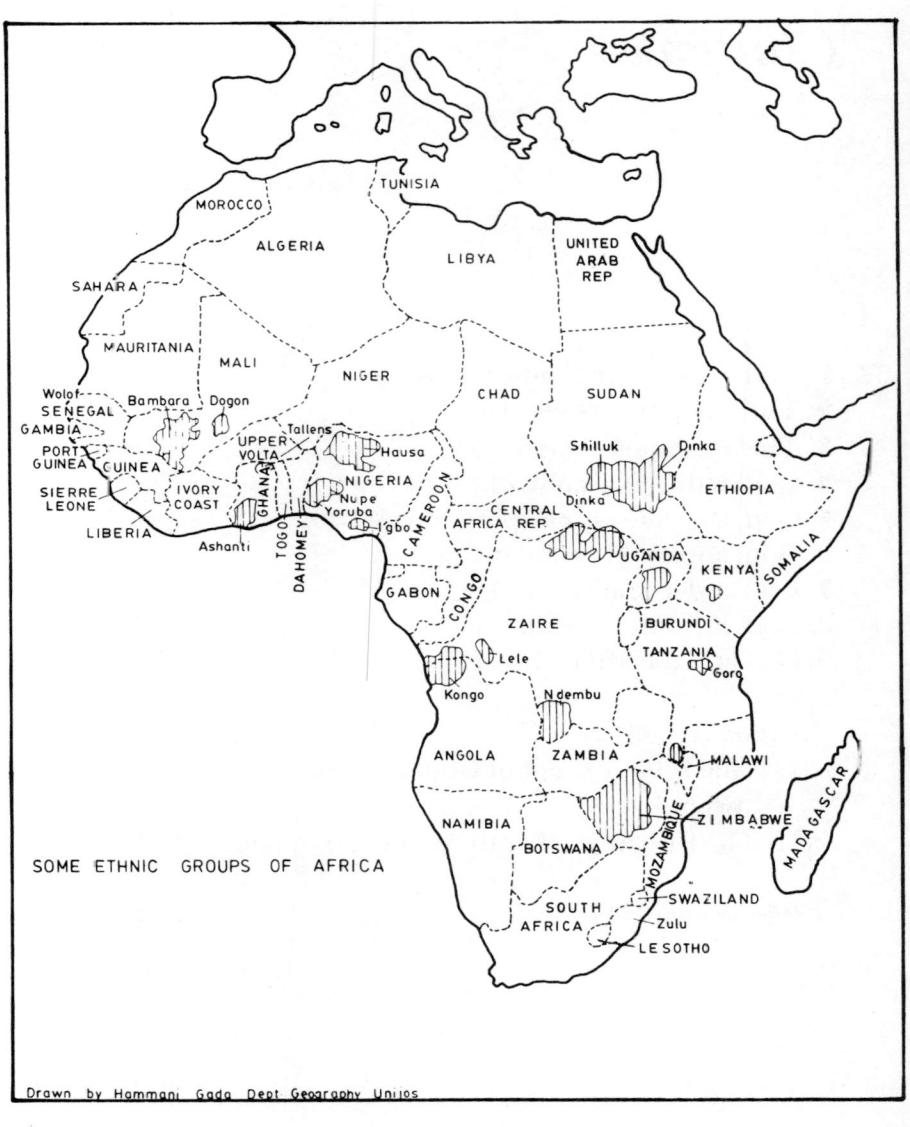

SOME ETHNIC GROUPS OF AFRICA

Drawn by Hammani Gada Dept Geography Unijos

Introduction

The long accepted thesis about traditional African religion
found its clearest but most extreme expression in the words
of Westermann, for whom 'Africa's God is a *deus incertus*
and a *deus remotus*'. This opinion has become fossilized in
the so-called 'withdrawal theory of God',[1] a withdrawal seen
in the attitude of unconcern with which He is said to be
treated. He is said to have no temples or shrines. No prayers
or sacrifices are made directly to Him.[2] It is a theory which
has also been applied to the Igbo beliefs about God.

In Basden's view, the influence of God on the life of the
Igbo is negligible. 'It is purely theoretical and has no
marked influence on life and character.'[3] Correia puts this
view more dramatically: *'Dieu existe bien, mais pourquoi
l'adorer? Il n'est pas méchant, c'est les diables qu'il faut
amadouer.'*[4] This view has been reiterated in different forms
by other writers on Igbo religion.[5] This book, however,
disputes this theory.

In the northern central part of Igboland, holding the
largest tribal group in south-eastern Nigeria, is a small
village called Ihembosi. This village is characterized by a
geographical feature which has had great appeal to the
Igbo religious mind – it is situated on top of a small, conical
hill and surrounded almost entirely by a level plain. This
geographical location has had far-reaching social and political consequences. Firstly, it limited the number of social,
cultural and economic contacts that Ihembosi could have
with the outside world. Secondly, being placed in such a
strategic position, the group succeeded in defending itself
and maintaining its independence against the much bigger
and hostile towns and villages which surrounded it.

But this geographical location has had an even greater

religious significance. The strategic position of Ihembosi was seen by its people not as a historical accident, but as a special favour from God. The common belief in Ihembosi and the surrounding country was that the hill was *Ugwu Chukwu*, God's hill, and the centre of the world itself. Ihembosi, they said, was on God's hill. This was, however, both its strength and its weakness. Ihembosi has had to remain a very small town because God's hill is a small place, yet it was always strong and defiant because of its position on God's hill. An elder from Ihembosi, Ezenwadeyi, explained this very beautifully in what sounds like a poetic language:

'We are told,
That we, the people of Ihembosi,
That we are at the peak of Chukwu's hill
That is how people speak of us,
And we go by that name
That we live on Chukwu's hill . . .
We are told that we live at the centre
It was what we are told
And every town says it,
That Ihembosi lives on Chukwu's hill
That Ihembosi lives at the centre,
The fact that we are on Chukwu's hill from of old
Is the secret
Of our success.'[6]

This ancient belief was ritually expressed in Ihembosi itself. A mound, called *Mkpu Chukwu*, God's mound, had been built at the top of the hill to represent the altar of God, and around *Mkpu Chukwu* were symbols of all the other deities worshipped in the town – even though they still had their own individual shrines in various parts of the town.

Each year at the harvest season, the whole town assembled at the *Mkpu Chukwu* for an annual rite by which God was worshipped. The rite was called *Igba Mkpu Chukwu*, celebrating the altar of God. The head of the village presided over the rite and the elders sat round the shrine for the *Igo Ofo*, offering of prayers and blessings. Then followed a sacrifice of fowls and new yams, after which there was rejoicing and dancing. Throughout the year, however, most of the acts of worship were offered to the deities and local spirits at their own shrines.

THE ECOLOGY OF THE IGBO CULTURE AREA

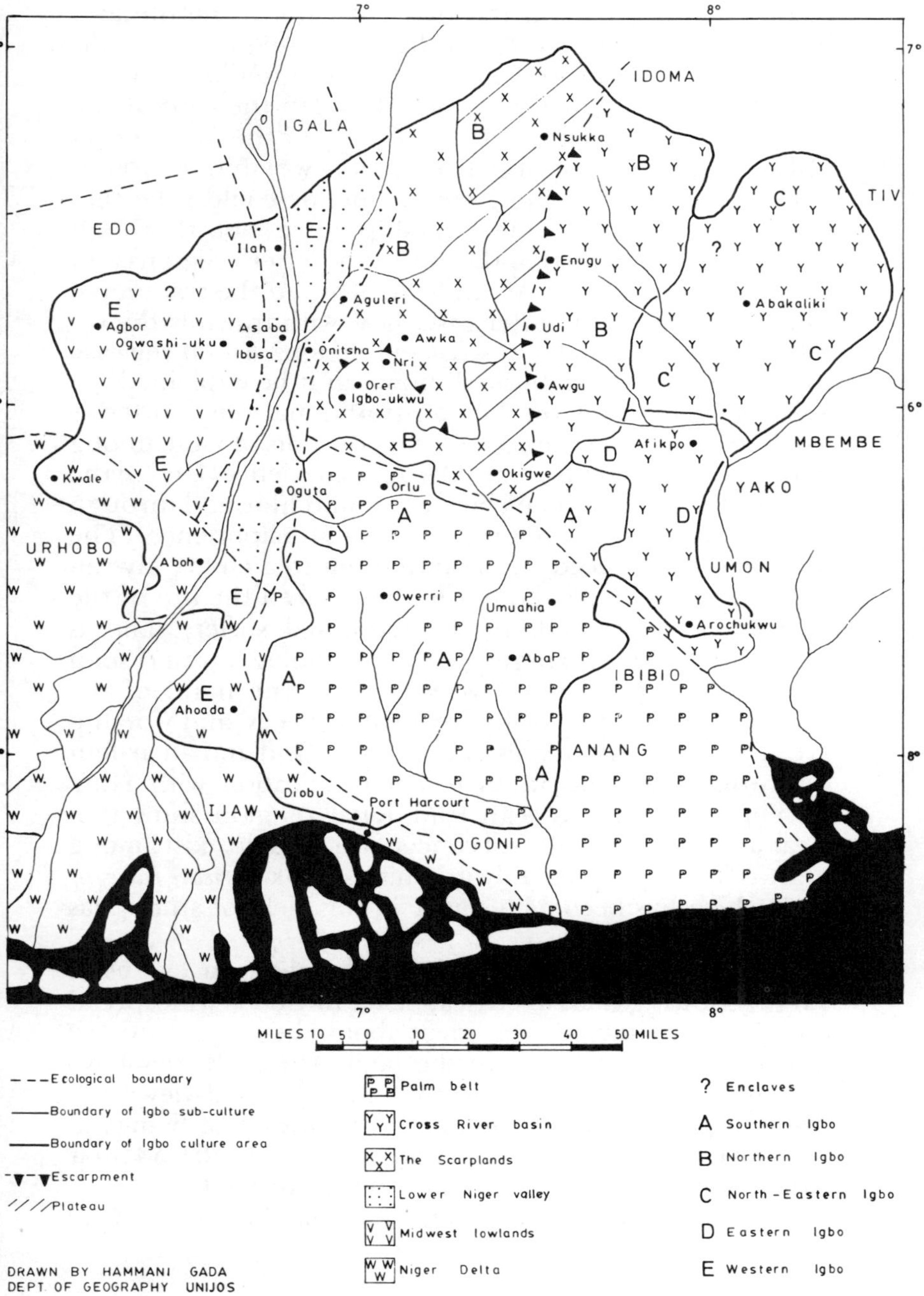

IDOMA

IGALA

B ·Nsukka ▲ Y B Y C Y TIV

EDO

E ·Ilah

?B

·Enugu

·Abakaliki

E ·Agbor V Asaba ·Aguleri ·Udi B C C
Ogwashi-uku V Ibusa ·Onitsha ·Awka
·Nri
·Orer ·Awgu
·Igbo-ukwu B

MBEMBE

E B D ·Afikpo YAKO

·Kwale Oguta ·Orlu Okigwe A D UMON

URHOBO

·Aboh E A P
·Owerri ·Umuahia Y ·Arochukwu

E ·Ahoada A ·Aba IBIBIO

A ANANG

·Diobu ·Port Harcourt

IJAW OGONI

MILES 10 5 0   10   20   30   40   50 MILES

- - - Ecological boundary
——— Boundary of Igbo sub-culture
———— Boundary of Igbo culture area
▼▼ Escarpment
/// Plateau

DRAWN BY HAMMANI GADA
DEPT OF GEOGRAPHY UNIJOS

P P / P P	Palm belt
Y Y	Cross River basin
X X	The Scarplands
...	Lower Niger valley
V V V	Midwest lowlands
W W W	Niger Delta

? Enclaves

A Southern Igbo

B Northern Igbo

C North-Eastern Igbo

D Eastern Igbo

E Western Igbo

The rite of *Igba Mkpu Chukwu* at Ihembosi raises fundamental questions about the place of God in the life and
habits of worship of the Igbo religion; consequently, it calls
into question the aforementioned generalization concerning African traditional religion. How can the case of the
Ihembosi be reconciled with the theory of the 'withdrawal
of God'? Are cases of organized public worship of God in
Africa exceptions to the general rule, or could it be that
field-work reports of no worship were not thorough
enough? Could it be that the spread of other religions and
external influences in Africa have affected the traditional
worship of God? In either case, how withdrawn is the so-
called 'withdrawn God' in African religion? And if the case
for withdrawal is established, how can it be explained?

No serious writer on African traditional religion today
would doubt the existence of clear concepts of God among
many African peoples. The African experiences God in the
most striking phenomena he sees around him, and through
His manifestation in nature and human experience. 'The
Supreme Being needs no pointing out to a child', says an
Ashanti proverb. Anybody who has shared the life of the
African as it is lived in his traditional society, and is
acquainted with his language and psychology, would soon
discover that God looms very large in the mind of the
African. Everyday speech, proverbs, prayers, and worship
are all imbued with man's awareness of God and an ardent
desire to enter into intimate communication with Him.
Recent studies in African traditional religion show that
clear and highly developed concepts of God do exist among
most African peoples. Edwin Smith's book *African Ideas of
God*, which has become a classic in this field of study, has
established this.[7]

In two inspiring books, Mbiti has made an extensive
survey showing that, in Africa, belief in God is widespread
and there are indeed clear ideas about His nature and His
attributes.[8] Contributors to the book *African Worlds* have
shown that God is central to the African world-view:[9] the
origin of the universe, the inter-relationship of beings in
the universe, the purpose and end of man's life all find their
explanation in the existence and power of God.

Yet one has to contend with the fact that the worship God

receives is not in proportion with His position in their system of belief. *A priori*, one could say that it is an anomaly for any group to have clear ideas about God and His rôle in the universe and still, consciously or unconsciously, allow these concepts very little impact on their daily lives and worship. The explanations usually given are that God is seen as the ultimate force in the universe, and so is the ultimate recipient of whatever acts of worship are addressed to the intermediate deities. Secondly, it is suggested that the African approaches God through the subordinate deities because he finds the transcendence of God too perplexing, and is consequently at a loss as to how to approach Him. In approaching Him through the deities therefore, the African is only complying with his traditional etiquette, that of approaching a chief through his subordinate chiefs – who are closer to him and have his confidence. The third reason suggested is that 'Chukwu is good and does harm to no man – hence no need to worry about Him'.[10]

Bearing these observations in mind, one has to reckon with the fact that organized public worship of God *has* been discovered in a number of African societies. The Dogon of the Republic of Mali have public altars at which regular worship is offered. The Kikuyu have sacred groves where rams without blemish are sacrificed to God at specified periods.[11] Among the Ashanti of Ghana, temples dedicated to God existed in the palaces of chiefs, with altars and priests both dedicated to His service for life. Most homes also had altars at which offerings were made to Him.[12] Is it not then reasonable to suppose that the incidences of organized worship of God in Africa have not been fully documented? In fact, Fr. Arazu who discovered the festival of *Igba Mkpu Chukwu* in Ihembosi commented that although Ihembosi was his home town, and he had lived there most of his life, this festival only came to his notice by chance a few years ago because of a dispute as to who would preside at the ritual on that particular occasion.

Today, in Ihembosi, because of the drift from traditional religion to the Christian churches, the *Mkpu Chukwu*, God's mound, is in ruins and the annual communal worship has ceased. But God's shrines still exist in some homes and further to the north, in the Nsukka area, public communal shrines of God are found in the central markets of many villages, and sacrifices are offered there during the *Ime Chukwu*, God's festival, an annual festival in honour of the High God, Ezechitoke.

This book, then, is a study of the place of God in the life and worship of the Igbo of Nigeria. Its scope is extended to see what light the Igbo experience throws on the persisting problem of the place of God Himself in African traditional religion. In order to determine how much light the conclusions throw on the observations and objections raised about African beliefs about God, I have considered the following questions: Is the concept of the 'Supreme Being' in Africa one of a living God or a cosmic 'mana', as Driberg objects.[13] Is Chukwu 'a withdrawn God' as Uchendu claims, or is He also immanent in the world?[14] Are the norms of human conduct referred to God as their source and final arbiter? How does God determine man's hopes and aspirations in the after-life? Should one agree with Correia that the concept of the 'Supreme Being' found among the Igbo is due to Christian missionary influence?

I have tried to study African traditional religion as a theological system rather than as a set of anthropological facts. Religion, wherever it is found, tries to regulate the relationship between man and his God. I have therefore attempted to organize long-accepted Igbo beliefs about God – and their related beliefs – into a coherent body.

It is hoped that this book will also fill the gap in Igbo studies noted by Forde and Jones a generation ago: 'No full study of Igbo religion has been made, and available accounts of even the formal subjects of beliefs and cults are incomplete'.[15] Interest in the study of African traditional religion is growing in Nigeria and students and teachers should find this systematic study helpful.

The Igbo occupy a large part of South-eastern Nigeria and a small strip of land on the western bank of the river Niger. In Nigeria's present administrative structure, the Igbo are found in the Anambra, Imo, Rivers and Bendel states. They may now number about twelve million people.[16] 'The Igbo are a single people in the sense that they speak a number of related dialects, occupy a continuous tract of territory and have many features of social structure and culture in common, but they were not formerly politically unified.'[17] The village-group locally called 'town' was the largest political group. This was made up of a group of segmentary lineages, *Obi* or *Nsu,* and kindreds, *Umunna,* whose cohesion was maintained by interest in a common land, common shrines, a central market and the need to ward off attacks from their neighbours. Because of its high density of population – some towns have several thousand people – the clan is the widest ritual group. Its members, who may inhabit different towns, meet periodically to carry out ancestral or other rituals. The Igbo were sedentary agriculturists, though large numbers have now emigrated to towns in response to modernization. Western education is very popular and conversion to Christianity is high, while Islam has made no significant impact.

I have not only first-hand information of the beliefs and practices discussed here, but have actually lived and practised some of them. Although I was brought up as a Christian, I lived in a community where traditional religion still had a very strong hold. As a boy, I often joined my uncles and aunts in traditional rites and cults. My grandfather was an Ezeana – a priest of *Ala*, Earth Deity, whom tradition holds as custodian and authentic interpreter of traditional beliefs and customs. My father was his page from 1910 to 1916 and supplied me with much of the information used in this book. I gathered still more of my original material from a study of the journals and correspondence of the first missionaries who settled in Igboland from 1857 onwards. These documents are conserved in the archives of the Church Missionary Society in London. I also found much valuable information in the reports of British colonial administrators, now preserved in the National Archives at Enugu. Many of these documents include monographs on the religious beliefs of the peoples of Southern Nigeria, including the Igbo, and information gained from them alone shows that most of what is said here of the Igbo would also apply to most other peoples of Southern Nigeria. Some of the beliefs are almost identical, varying only in detail.

Finally, I personally tape-recorded interviews with surviving adherents of the traditional religion including priests, diviners, medicine-men, titled men and elders. These interviews were made over a period of four years, mostly in Anambra State. During this time, I had ample opportunity to reflect upon and cross-check my information and conclusions. My knowledge of the Igbo language has made it possible for me to gather much information from the rich store of their oral cultural traditions and throughout this book there are myths, proverbs, sayings, names and songs, many of which contain important information about Igbo religious beliefs.

I am greatly indebted to Prof. E. G. Parrinder, my teacher of African Traditional Religion at the School of Oriental and African Studies, who has continued to follow with very keen interest the continuing research which has resulted in this book. I will ever be grateful for the great inspiration and encouragement I have received from this great scholar. My gratitude goes to many pioneer authors whose toil and sweat have made it possible for Igbo traditional religious beliefs to be documented in the past. Without their contribution it would have been very difficult to ascertain some of the authentic beliefs in view of the tide of change sweeping through the Igbo country. Finally, I drew a wealth of information from a number of unpublished theses presented by Igbo Roman Catholic priests at different European universities, and I am most indebted to them all.

To Dr. Landy and Fr. Mackenna, who not only read and corrected my manuscript but gave me some valuable suggestions, I express my deep-felt thanks. I am greatly indebted to Dr. Okechukwu Njoku, and the staff of the National Museum, Jos, for the photographs of some of the Igbo works of art and for the use of their rich library. Last but not least, I must thank Mr. N.A. Ogugua who typed the manuscript.

Emefie Ikenga Metuh, University of Jos

Some colonial records and earlier books have 'Ibo' as the name of the tribe, but the people and neighbouring tribes know them as the 'Igbo'. This version has been retained throughout this book except in quotations. Relevant documents from these collections are listed in the Bibliography.

Notes

1 Westermann, D. *Africa and Christianity* (1937) p.74.
2 O'Connell, J. 'The Withdrawal of the High God in West African Religion: an essay of interpretation' *Man* 42, Article 109 (1962) p.67.
3 Basden, G. T. *Niger Ibos* (London, 1966 ed.) p.37.
4 Correia, Alves 'L'Animisme Ibo et les Divinités de la Nigéria', *Anthropos* 16–17 (1921–1922) p.361.
5 Forde, Daryll and Jones, G. I. *The Ibo and Ibibio-speaking peoples of South-eastern Nigeria* (1962) p.25.
6 Arazu, R. 'The Pagan', unpublished MS. A tape-recorded interview of an Igbo elder called Ezenwadeyi.
7 Smith, E. W. *African Ideas of God* (London, Edinburgh House Press, 1961).
8 Mbiti, J. S. *African Religions and Philosophy* (1971) p.83. *Concepts of God in Africa* (1970) p.56.
9 Forde, Daryll (ed.) *African Worlds* (Oxford University Press, 1968).
10 Arinze, F. A. *Sacrifice in Ibo Religion* (Ibadan, 1970) p.11.
11 Parrinder, E. G. *African Traditional Religion* (2nd revised ed., 1962) pp.37–38.
12 Parrinder, E. G. *West African Religion* (1969 ed.) p.15.
13 Driberg, J. H. 'The Secular Aspects of Ancestor Worship in Africa,' supplement to *Journal of the Royal African Society*, Vol. 35, No. 38 (Jan. 1936). Quoted by Smith, E. W. in *African Ideas of God*, p.21.
14 Uchendu, V. C. *The Igbo of Southeast Nigeria* (New York, 1965) p.94.
15 Forde, Daryll and Jones, G. I. op. cit. (1962) p.25.
16 Ekanem, I. *The 1963 Nigerian Census; A Critical Appraisal* (Benin City, r.p. 1972) p.67: Table on Distribution by Ethnic Groups; cf. *The Population Census*

of Nigeria (1973) Vol. 3, p.10. According to the 1963 census figures the Igbo numbered over 9.2 million.
17 Forde, Daryll and Jones, G. I. op. cit. (1962) p.95.

1 God in the cosmogonic myths

Africans do not have systematic doctrines on the origin of God or the origin of the universe, but they do have stories which tell of the beginning of things. These stories, in a very simple way, attempt to explain the origin of some of the fundamental realities of African experience and culture. Did this visible world have any beginning? How did the world come into existence? What is the origin of the things in the world itself? What is the origin of man, the beasts, mountains, rivers, forests and so forth? What of the deities? Had they, too, a beginning? What is the origin of God? The synthesis of the answers Africans have given to these – and their related questions – may be referred to as their theogony and cosmogony. A full account of African beliefs about the origin of matter can only be obtained by examining every aspect of the African's beliefs and his culture, but these are condensed in the creation stories and cosmogonic myths.

These narratives have been handed down to us in the form of myths and therefore speak in mythical language. Before I go on to retell some of these stories, it would be useful to repeat some of the observations that experts have made about the nature and function of myths in the religion of pre-literate societies. This provides a useful framework for the analysis of the African myths and the assessment of their religious content. I shall then examine a collection of the cosmogonic myths of the Igbo of Nigeria in order to discover the depth of religious belief woven into their explanation of the origin of the universe.

One of the perennial problems in dealing with mythology is the value to be attached to mythical narratives. Are myths authentic vehicles of a people's concept of nature and the world around them? To what extent do myths contain a valid expression of their religious beliefs, tribal world-view, traditional laws and norms of morality? Lévy-Bruhl, in *Les Fonctions Mentales dans les Sociétés inférieures*, thinks that 'primitive men' (usually non-Europeans) are incapable of purely abstract reflections and consequently their myths are merely rôle stories without thought or logic, devised simply as forms of entertainment.[1] Many authors, however, strongly disagree with this view. Malinowski noted that the natives of the Trobriand Islands clearly distinguish myths, *liliu*, from folk tales on the one hand and from legends on the other. Whereas folk tales were told for amusement and legend 'opens up past historical vistas', myths (which he calls 'sacred tales') come into play 'when rite, ceremony, or a social or moral rule demands justification, warrant of antiquity, reality and sanctity'.[2]

The Igbo recognize these three different types of narrative and have a different name for each. Folk tales (which have acquired the name 'moonlight stories' in West Africa because they are told for entertainment on moonlit nights) are called by the Igbo '*Akikọ-ifo*', stories with songs; legends which tell the history of the distant past are called '*Akikọ Gboo*', stories about the past, while myths are called '*Akikọ ọdi N'ala*', literally narratives about tradition, which tell sacred history.

Many writers have emphasized the importance of myths in the study of the beliefs of pre-literate peoples. Malinowski has described myth in primitive culture as a 'pragmatic charter for primitive faith and moral wisdom'. He even thinks that 'myth is to the savage what, to a fully believing Christian, is the biblical story of Creation, of the Fall, of the Redemption of Christ's Sacrifice on the Cross'.[2] Hermann Baumann studied 2,500 African myths and arrived at a similar conclusion. He thinks that 'a myth is the clear presentation of the outlook of life of people living in communities. It is their objective and permanent philosophy of life'.[3] Myths definitely do tell us about certain realities – including religious truths. A people's understanding of their environment, their geography, history, medicine and their social and political institutions could very easily be revealed in their myths.

Some of these are popular stories and draw from facts and ideas already familiar to the people themselves – their environment, pattern of life and ideas of God and the mystical forces which influence man. Thus one would expect that the myths of desert peoples would mirror desert surroundings and the conditions of desert life. Similarly, myths of agriculturists, fruit-gatherers, pastoral peoples, those with simple societies and those with centralized government would variously reflect these different situations. This enhances their value as authentic vehicles of religious beliefs, since such beliefs would enjoy an appreciable degree of authenticity. In pre-literate societies this rôle is seen as being very important, because in the absence of writing, myths are among the most effective means of conserving, preserving and transmitting religious beliefs. The creation myths in the book of Genesis, for example, contain many fundamental religious beliefs on which is based the development of the history of salvation throughout the Bible.

Some myths like the Nri myth to be discussed later are ritual texts or creeds; they are believed to confer on the candidate the mystical powers attached to the office. When used at rituals such as priestly or kingly consecrations or initiation rites, they are believed to have a sacramental character. One can therefore conclude that, in general, the religious beliefs contained in myths enjoy a high degree of authenticity, though this could be contested in particular cases. The study of myths is therefore essential for the understanding of the rôle of religion in traditional African societies.

It must not be presumed, however, that the whole body of a people's beliefs about God is contained in their myths. Even in myths which tell about God, the information they give about him and his relationship with the world is limited by the scope of the myth itself. This is evident from the three Igbo myths which follow.

Creation myths

The first myth, which is contained in an esoteric ritual text of the Nri, a priestly clan among the northern Igbo, is primarily concerned with establishing the right claimed by the king of Nri to receive tributes from other clans.[4] The myth vests its claim in the authority of *Chukwu*, God, which it presumed its audience would recognize and accept. Although this myth is of the religious-dogmatic genre, the information it actually gives about God and certain other religious beliefs is very limited. Similarly, the second myth is a cosmogonic myth and discusses God's rôle in bringing the world into existence. It was recovered by Horton at Ibagwa, another northern Igbo group, and represents a popular belief about how the world began.[5] The third myth is the creed of an Igbo group of the Niger delta.[6]

1 Chukwu and Eze Nri (God and the King of Nri)

In the extracts from his journal of October 1878, Perry writes of the Nri: 'They were, as it were, the Levites of the Ibo people who dwell in these parts; in fact their influence extends to Igara, and all the kings and chiefs of this way are crowned or consecrated by them.'[7] From time immemorial till the present day, the itinerant Nri priests have had the exclusive right to perform certain rituals among some Igbo groups. Only they have the power to establish and abolish taboos of the Earth goddess, *Isubi Nso Ala*. Only they could cleanse one from abominations, *Aru*. They have the final say in interpreting traditions, *Ikowa Odinala*, and the rites of title-taking, *Ichi-Echichi*. The influence of the Nri was based on the ritual authority generated by this myth which claims that the Eze Nri received from Chukwu magico-religious powers over the forces that control the fertility of the land, smallpox epidemics, and pestilence.[8] The origin of certain essential foods and some Igbo social and economic institutions are due to a revelation which Chukwu, the High God, made to Eze Nri, the divine King. The myth runs thus: Eri, father of Nri, and Namaku his wife were sent down by Chukwu, a sky God. When Eri came down from the sky, he had to stand on an ant-heap as all the land was then a morass. He complained to Chukwu, who thereupon sent him an *Awka*, blacksmith, to dry up the land. While Eri

Plate 1 Reconstruction of a burial chamber of Eze Nri from Igbo-Ukwu excavations, dated ninth century A.D. (From *Igbo-Ukwu: Account of Archaeological Discoveries in Eastern Nigeria* (Faber, London, 1970), by permission of the author, Thurstan Shaw)

lived, he and his dependants were fed by Chukwu and their food was *Azụ Igwe*, fish from heaven. When Eri died, this food supply ceased, so Nri complained to Chukwu, but was told that in order to get food he would have to kill and bury his eldest son and daughter. When Nri objected, Chukwu promised to send *Dioka* from the sky, to carve the *ichi* or facial cicatrization marks on the foreheads of the two children. (Dioka was the founder of the Umudioka clan who still practise the 'trade' throughout Igboland to this day.) After Dioka arrived and cut the *ichi* on the faces of the two children, Nri cut their throats and buried them in separate graves.

Three native weeks later (twelve days), shoots appeared from the graves of these two children. From the grave of his son, Nri dug up a yam. He cooked and ate it and found it so pleasing that he fell into a sleep so deep that his family thought him dead. When he awoke, he told his astonished family what he had done. They, too, ate of the yam and also fell asleep. The next day, Nri dug up cocoyams from his daughter's grave, ate them and likewise slept again. This is why the yam is called the 'son of Nri', and the cocoyam called the 'daughter of Nri'. The firstborn son and daughter of Nri are marked to this day with the *ichi* to commemorate the event.

Nri also killed a male slave and a female slave and buried them in separate graves. After three native weeks (twelve days), an oil palm sprang from the grave of Nri's male slave, while a bread-fruit tree sprang from the grave of his female slave.

Then Chukwu ordered Nri to distribute these new foods to all mankind. Nri objected but Chukwu insisted. As a reward for doing so, Chukwu gave Nri the right of cleansing every town of the abominations, *Nsọ Ala*, committed in it, of crowning kings, of tying *Ngwulu*, ankle cords, on candidates for *Ọzọ*, titles. He and his successors would also have the privilege of making *ogwuji*, yam medicine, to ensure a plentiful yam harvest each year. In return for these services, all the surrounding towns would pay the Nri an annual tribute. Umunri, the descendants of Nri, could travel unarmed throughout the world and nobody would harm them.

Plate 2 Bronze mask worn on the chest by Eze Nri. Notice the
ichi facial marks. (From *Igbo-Ukwu: Account of Archaeological
Discoveries in Eastern Nigeria* (Faber, London, 1970), by
permission of the author, Thurstan Shaw)

Thus although Eri, Awka and Dioka were all sent down from the sky by Chukwu, only Eri and Nri actually obtained food from Chukwu.

The myth goes on to explain how some Igbo cultural institutions originated from the Nri. These include the Igbo four-day week and the names of the Igbo market-days. In the beginning the days of the week had no names, for there was no way of counting the days because the sun was always shining, and no one slept. Then four strangers arrived at Aguleri with four baskets. Nri asked Chukwu where they came from. Chukwu promised he would send somebody who would divulge their names and origins. A wise man called *Okpeta* appeared with a rat, *Oke*. At night, Okpeta tied a string around Oke and let it go into one of the baskets and make a noise. One of the unknown visitors, *ndi amaghi ahaha*, called out to one of his companions: *'Eke, Eke!'* and told him there was something in his basket. Okpeta quickly removed the rat, but took a note of the name. Then he let the rat fall into the second basket and a companion called out *'Oye! Oye!'* to the owner. Okpeta continued until he had found out the names of the other two visitors, *'Afo'* and *'Nkwo'* respectively. And these four men founded the four Igbo market-days. Sent by Chukwu, their four baskets contained fish and in this they traded. That was why they attracted Oke.[9]

2   Chukwu in the Ibagwa cosmogonic myth

Ibagwa is not as influential as the priestly Nri clan. Like most Igbo village-groups, it cherished its independence and developed its own customs and traditions, among which is this creation myth. Though not as sophisticated as the Nri myth, it is interesting to note that similar cosmic realities are mentioned in both – Chukwu, the sky, the sun, the earth, day and night, and the four days of the Igbo week. This may well be a characteristic feature of Igbo mythology.

According to this myth, Chukwu created the universe. He is *Oke Abiama* – maker of everything. He made the universe in two parts – Earth, *Ala* and Sky, *Igwe*, after which he created two messengers – the Sun, *Anyanwu* and Moon, *Qnwa* to travel across the sky, to bring Him back news of what happens on earth. The elders of Ibagwa illustrate this with a diagram which represents the universe as a circle divided by two diameters which cross each other at right angles. The diameters are traced by the journeys which the sun and the moon make across the world. This cosmic phenomenon is linked with the four deities after whom the Igbo four-day week was named, and with the sacredness of the number four in Igbo culture thus: 'Chukwu sees that the sun travels across the world in the daytime to cut it in two, but as the sun and moon travel in different parts, so the world is divided by Chukwu into four, so Chukwu created the four Igbo weekdays *Orie, Afq, Nkwq, Eke*. This is why the number four is sacred, *Nso*, to us.'[10]

3 A creation account from a Delta group

The Reverend M. Smart recorded this creation myth of an Igbo group in the Niger Delta region. It is brief but very interesting because it is a model Igbo creation account. It acknowledges that there exists 'one Supreme Being, the First Cause of all Things', but it indicates at the same time that because of his great distance in the heavens, he also created several inferior deities to superintend different parts of the universe. Among these divinities, *Adum* stands the first in order, and was the creator of the human race. The first man was called *Ban-to-lee* and the first woman was called *Koo-loo*.[11]

Theological conclusions from these myths

To make a true analysis and an objective evaluation of these myths, it is essential to consider not only their literary genre but also their scope. The first is in the form of a creed which itself is part of the esoteric ritual texts of the Umunri clan. According to Jeffreys, it is recited and re-enacted during the coronation ceremonies of the king, perhaps in the belief that the recital and re-enaction will confer on the king the magico-ritual and political powers which are associated with his office. In fact, as part of the coronation ceremonies, the king again mounts a special white ant-hill from which he prays to Chukwu and the ancestors. This re-enacts Eri's sojourn on an ant-hill after his descent from heaven. The king is fed with white clay, symbolizing the heavenly substance, *Azu Igwe*, with which Chukwu fed his ancestor before the discovery of earthly food. The king performs the miracle of the parting of the waters of the Anambra river with his *Ofo*, sacred staff, so that an attendant can collect some white clay from the river bed, from which his orb, *odudu*, would be moulded. This perhaps recreates Eri's drying up of the primordial waters from the surface of the earth. The myth is therefore not only 'sacred history', but when used as a ritual text, it also has a sacramental character.

Myths tell 'sacred history', therefore they discuss what is believed to have happened. But they also tell of 'sacred reality'. Hence, for the most part, the characters in these Igbo myths are not ordinary human beings; they are gods or culture heroes and as such they are credited with fantastic powers and sometimes, paradoxically, with obscene and immoral behaviour.[12]

In the first myth, for example, Eri, Nri, Dioka, Oke, Okpeta are all culture heroes and some of their deeds would be considered mysterious by normal human beings. Eri and Namaku were sent down from heaven and sat on an ant-hill. They were fed with *Azu Igwe*. The Awka blacksmith dries up the watery world with his bellows. Chukwu orders the killing of Nri's son and daughter. Nri, the first divine king, slaughters his children and slaves to get food, and so forth. These fantasies, however, must not obscure the deep religious truths contained in these myths.

The second myth emphasizes that Chukwu, God, is creator. He created the universe. Because of this, the Igbo give God the title *Oke Abiama*, maker of everything. The myth leaves us in no doubt about the universality of God's creative activity, for the greatest beings in the universe namely the Earth, *Ala*, the Sky, *Igwe*, the heavenly bodies and the Sun, *Anyanwu*, and the Moon, *Onwa*, are all creatures of God. Even small details of the Igbo culture – like their four-day week – are believed to have been created by God. It is God's arrangement of the journeys of sun and moon across the earth that gives rise not only to the four-day week, but also the sacredness of the number four itself.

But both myths fail to tell us what they actually mean by 'creation'. Is it creation from nothing, or was it from some pre-existing matter? There is no mention of any pre-existing matter. The Igbo word *Eke* used in the myth does, in fact, include the idea of 'creation from nothing' but the myths tell us nothing about the origin of God. Is Chukwu the first uncaused Cause? The myths do not say so but certainly presume it. God *is* presented as the creator of all things; if he is creator of all things, then he is not dependent on anything for his existence.

The third myth states categorically that God is the First Cause of all things. Even the deities are his creatures. He is One and Supreme. The concepts and the expressions used in this myth are so technical and philosophical that one wonders whether they are the ideas of the informants, or those of the reporters. But the basic teaching – that Chukwu is Creator of everything including deities and men – is clear and certainly authentic.

The first myth is not concerned with the creative rôle of God. It rather emphasizes that Chukwu is Lord of everything. This is understandable since the narrator is primarily concerned with justifying the powers and privileges claimed by *Eze Nri*, the Nri king. He did this by giving them the authority of the universal Lordship of Chukwu which all Igbo recognize. As Lord of heaven and earth, he sends down the first human pair to rule on earth. He has complete control over the natural forces. He orders the drying of the earth. He controls time, dividing it into night and day and into the four-day week. He has control over life and death: he orders Nri to kill his son and daughter. He shows himself even Lord of morality by ordering homicide, which the Igbo otherwise abhor as evil and immoral. He is Lord of all men, irrespective of their tribe or profession (Nri, Awka or Dioka). He is source and Lord of all human industry and culture. He sent Awka, the first blacksmith, who became the ancestor of the Awka clan, and Dioka, the first artist and ancestor of the Umudioka clan. Man is dependent on God for everything – even for his food.

But many fundamental questions about God and His relationship with the world are still left unresolved. This myth tells us nothing either about the origin of Chukwu or the world. In fact, the existence of the earth described as a morass preceded Chukwu's intervention. Chukwu therefore appears more as an organizer than a creator. But Nri is a demiurge, a subordinated creator. This must be attributed to the scope of the myth and in no way disproves what has been said about the creative rôle of Chukwu. In fact, the integral message of the myth seems to be condensed in this phrase from the Nri narrator: 'Thus Eri, Awka and Diọka have all come from the sky, sent down by Chukwu, but it was Eri who obtained food from Chukwu.'

Each of the three myths in its own way stresses that Chukwu is the organizer of the world. He made the world habitable. He gives the world new crops. He creates night and day and arranges them into the four days of the Igbo week. He creates deities to superintend the different parts of the universe. Thus not only the material world but its most important attributes – space, motion, time and order – are introduced and controlled by God.

The first and third myths mention that the first human pair was sent down or created by God. Far from confirming the opinion expressed by Danquah that 'Akan Knowledge of God teaches that He is a Great Ancestor',[13] this establishes the opposite view. God is not an ancestor but creator of the first ancestors. No family relationship between God and the first human pair is expressed or implied in these myths.

Other cosmogonic myths

There are many other Igbo myths about the origin of the world and of some of man's major experiences in life. The paradox of optimism and frustration, of life and death, of joy and sorrow, of good and evil in the world is as intriguing to the Igbo as it is to the rest of mankind. The Igbo know that God is the Creator and Lord of everything, a benevolent protector and a generous benefactor to mankind, but they are frustrated when they find Him difficult to approach and *impossible to comprehend*. They are desperate when they see His immense powers and infinite goodness and yet are unable to harness these powers to solve the many problems which continue to plague them in life. They find themselves in the ironic situation of those who, as the Igbo proverb says, 'wash their hands with spittle in the middle of the ocean'. They know that God made life; whence, therefore, is death? They know that God is good and made everything good; how is it then that evil came into the world? Some Igbo myths try to explain these paradoxes by tracing the origin of man's difficulty in approaching God. Others explain the advent of death in the world. Still others trace the origins of evil.

The withdrawal of God

One of the characteristic features of African traditional religion is that God is usually approached through the intermediary of the deities and the ancestors and rarely through direct worship. This has led to the extreme view which calls the African God the 'Withdrawn God', a *Deus otiosus*, inactive God, or a *Deus absconditus*, hidden God.[14] Myths from several parts of Africa refer to a golden age when God was near and accessible to man, but later withdrew into the distant skies because of the faults of some men or beasts, and appear to bear out this theory. A similar Igbo myth attributes God's withdrawal to the fault of man.

In the beginning, God was living very close to man. Men were able to approach Him whenever they liked and He was quite willing to solve all their problems and supply all their needs. But men became very mischievous and gave God no rest. Every tiny complaint was brought to Him – any problem no matter how trivial, God must hear of it. A lost broom, a broken hoe, domestic quarrels all were brought before God. At last Chukwu could take no more. Men were taking Him too much for granted and He felt he needed to do other things besides settling human problems. So, in disgust, God withdrew far, far above into the heavens. Man can still reach Him, but only through the intermediary of the deities and ancestors, or through certain rites and rituals.

Tempting as the theory of the withdrawal of God is, this book does not subscribe to it. It is a hastily drawn conclusion about African traditional religion, hitherto universally accepted, which should now be rejected in the face of over-whelming evidence to the contrary.[15] The withdrawal of God as referred to in the myths must not be taken too literally. They only try to explain the universal human experience of divine transcendence. Abundant evidence of God's immanence exists in Igbo traditional religion and the conflict between the transcendence and the immanence of God is as much a feature of African traditional religion as of other religions. The following two myths seem to suggest that Igbo religion has achieved some balance between God's transcendence and immanence. The first explains the advent of death.

The coming of death

This is the theme of many African myths. Death is pre-sented as a challenge to God, who created the world to be a good and happy place. Most African myths agree that death was not present in the beginning, but came much later after God's creative act, and must have been the result of man's sin or due to a mistake on the part of some other creature. With death, the greatest and the most feared of all evils, came all the other evils.

One Igbo myth tells us that in the beginning there was no death. When people began to die, men were very worried and sent a dog to tell God that whenever a man died, he should be restored to life. On the way, the dog fell asleep, and was overtaken by a toad who had overheard the message. He reached God first and told Him that men desired that when they died, they should have no wish to return to the world again. Chukwu welcomed the toad's message and decided that death would be the end of man's sojourn on earth. Thus, although a human being may rein-carnate, he comes back with a different body, a different consciousness and a different *Chi*.

The coming of evil

Another Igbo myth tells of the advent of evil. According to this one, in the beginning there was no evil in the world. Men had everything they needed and whenever they wanted anything, they sent a messenger to Chukwu, who supplied it. On one occasion the vulture, then a beautiful, powerful bird, was sent to Chukwu on just such an errand. Chukwu gave the vulture a big parcel to bring back to mankind, but warned the bird of the serious consequences which would result if he opened the parcel in mid-air before arriving on earth.

The vulture disobeyed God, and a very heavy rain and all sorts of evil descended upon the earth and claimed the vulture as its first victim. That is why the vulture is now so haggard and dirty. Ever since, he has been trying – without success – to clean up the world which he polluted, by eating up all dead and decaying matter. Hence the Igbo proverbs: *Achuọaja, afụgh udene, imara na ihe mere be ndi mmụọ*, 'If a sacrifice to the spirits is made, and a vulture does not come to devour it, it is certain that things are not well in the spirit-world'.

Each of the myths referred to here, recognizes God as Creator and Providence of the whole world. At the same time, each recognizes that certain negative features in the world cannot be reconciled with this rôle. How could God be a creator and a provident father and yet be unapproachable? How could God create men only to let them die? How could a good God produce an evil world? The myths seem to say the same thing: things were not so from the beginning. Something went wrong somewhere and God is not to blame. The withdrawal myths say men were to blame; God withdrew because men abused their early freedom to approach Him. Death was not in the world from the beginning. But God is not to blame for its advent. The mythical dog, *Nkita*, is to blame. Had he been more responsible in attitude, things would have been quite different. The toad, *Awọ*, bears even greater blame. He was jealous because men chose the dog to carry the great message of immortality to God. Even men themselves are not completely without blame for the unfortunate outcome. They should have chosen the safest, if not the fastest means to carry a message of such far-reaching importance. Nor is God to blame for the presence of evil in the world. God originally created everything good and sent men only good things, so the presence of evil is blamed on the disobedience and curiosity of the vulture.

Summary and conclusions

Thus, from Igbo mythology, we can already reconstruct a rough sketch of Igbo theodicy. All the myths discussed here presume that the existence of God is a well-known and indisputable fact. There is no attempt to assert or defend God's existence. The other statements made in the myths hinge on this. The mystery of the existence of the world, the coming into existence of man, of the seasons, the deities and the fundamental human institutions (lineages, marriage, market-days and so forth), even the mystery of the unfortunate presence of death and evil in the world are so overwhelming that it becomes absolutely necessary to postulate the existence of God to explain them.

The myths do tell us something about God Himself, but not very much. God precedes everything in existence; He depends on nothing for His existence. He is therefore *Ens a se*, He exists of Himself. He is Creator of everything, Lord of everything. He continues to preserve everything in existence, which therefore depends on Him for its continued existence. He is the Great Providence, *Chukwu*. God is all-powerful; He knows everything; He is all-good; He is in no way evil and cannot will evil. Death, and the evil in the world cannot be traced to him. He is kind and merciful. Above all *He is a person*, and listens and understands and often grants our requests. He is somehow aloof from men, but this is not an essential part of his nature. It came about due to man's own misconduct. God's transcendence does not contradict His immanence.

We can therefore conclude that there is a vast resource of traditional religious beliefs in the African cosmogonies. Some could well provide clues as to how some of the problems which beset studies in African traditional religion could be solved. Is African traditional religion deistic or theistic? What is the relationship between God and the deities? Is traditional religion monotheistic or polytheistic? What is the African sense of morality? Many of these and other questions have not been answered satisfactorily. It is equally true to say that vast resources of data already documented from sources of the oral tradition have yet to be tapped. In this sense, there is still much work to be done in the studying of African traditional religion.

Notes

1 Lévy-Bruhl, L. *Les Fonctions Mentales dans les Sociétés inférieures* (2nd ed., 1912) pp.30ff.
2 Malinowski, B. 'Myths in primitive Society' in *Magic, Science and Religion* (1954) p.107.
3 Baumann, Hermann *Schöpfung und Urzeit des Menschen im Mythus der Africanischen Völker* (1936). Quoted by Smith, E. W. *African Ideas of God* (1961) p.6.
4 Jeffreys, M. D. W. 'The Umundri Tradition of Origin' *African Studies* 15 (3 Sept. 1956) pp.119–131.
5 Horton, W. R. C. 'God, Man, and the Land in a Northern Ibo Village-Group', *Africa*, 26 (Jan.1956) p.18.
6 CA3/035/7 Niger Missions, 'Journal Excerpts' by W. Smart, Bonny 1868-76.
7 CA3/030/1–11 Niger Missions, 'Reports' of Rev. Solomon S. Perry, Native Pastor, Onitsha, 1872–1880.
8 Onwuejeogwu, M. A. 'An Ethno-Historical Survey of Igbo West and East of the Lower Niger', unpublished MS (1969).
    Cf. Alutu, J. *A Groundwork of Nnewi History* (1963), p.171. Some outdated customs were abrogated in Nnewi in 1930, by Eze Nri.
9 Jeffreys, M. D. W. op. cit. (1956) p.121. Several authors have investigated the Umunri traditions before and after Jeffreys. Thomas, N. W. *Anthropological Report on the Ibo-speaking Peoples,* I (London, 1914) p.55. Cf. Onwuejeogwu, M. A. op. cit. (1969). My own research which includes interviews of several Agwukwu elders

confirms that Jeffreys' account is the most authentic.
10 Horton, W. R. C. op. cit. (1956) p.18.
11 CA3/035/7 Niger Missions, 'Journal Excerpts' by W. Smart, Bonny 1868–76.
12 Turner, V. W. 'Myth and Symbol', in *International Encyclopedia of the Social Sciences*, Vol.10 (1969). Turner here remarks that in myths just as in the 'Rites of passage', one finds the most sacred mixed with the most profane, the most obscene, and the most immoral. In many theogonies and cosmogonies the deities and heroes mate incestuously, devour one another and clearly transgress human and cultural norms of equity and justice. This he calls the *liminal* character of myths.
13 Danquah, J. B. *The Akan Doctrine of God* (London, 1944) p.45.
14 Westermann, D. *Africa and Christianity* (1937) p.74.
15 Metuh, E. E. 'The Supreme God in Igbo Life and Worship' *Journal of Religion in Africa* Vol. V.

2 The names for God

The Romans had a saying: *Nomen est omen*, 'a name is an omen'. The Igbo share this conviction. Names are not just identification marks put on people. Every Igbo name has a meaning, and people are not given their names in haste, for the name is supposed to represent the most cherished thought in the mind of the giver at the time the name is given. Much reflection and heart-searching takes place before the naming ceremony – usually a very elaborate and festive occasion. The genius and the achievements of great men can sometimes be read in the names given to their children and grand-children. For example, my grand-father initially had great difficulty in getting a male child. After spending a great deal of money in marrying many wives, consulting oracles and *dibia*, fortune-tellers, and making remedies, he succeeded at long last with his third wife. Accordingly, he named his first son *Olisanumba*, 'God does not hear reproaches', as if to say that one cannot force God's hand. My father, who was the fifth son, he named *Ikenga* after the deity who brings success, to indicate that his lineage was now firmly established. He acquired wealth and decided to take the *Ataka* title, the highest and costliest in our clan, so he called his seventh son – born at that time – *Ekwelumeze*, 'I have decided to take the kingly title'. The title cost him twenty cows, so he named his eighth son *Udefi*, 'amidst the cry of cows', i.e. a son born when cows are plentiful.

It is necessary to delve more deeply into the significance of names in Igbo culture to fully appreciate the wealth of knowledge which can be drawn from the names they give to God. As we have said, the Igbo believe that there is a very close link between a person and his name, such that the

Igbo believe that if you know a person's name, you can exert certain influences over him. Conversely, charms cannot harm anybody whose name is unknown no matter how near or otherwise well-known he might be to his enemy. Spirits whose names are not known cannot be invoked or placated; such spirits are regarded as evil and can only be driven away by the rites of *Ichu Aja*, exorcism. A name expresses a person's personality and the Igbo therefore try to give names which represent as accurately as possible the essential nature of the person to whom the name is given. This is very well illustrated by the practice of *Igba Agu*, identifying the namesake. Most children are believed to be the reincarnation of an ancestor or a local deity. If the identity of the ancestor cannot be easily recognized through certain visible characteristics, it is necessary to hold the rite of *Igba Agu* to identify the personality incarnate in the baby, for example, the name *Nne Nna* – paternal grandmother (come back).

A name may also commemorate a historical event e.g. *Nwogu*, a son born during war. It may express the parents' state of mind, e.g. *Eyiuche*, 'the unexpected child'. It may express a religious sentiment or belief like *Chukwuemeka*, 'God is very kind'. It may affirm a moral, religious or philosophical truth like *Nwakaego*, 'a child is more valuable than money'; *Ndidi Amaka*, 'patience is very good'. According to H. A. Wieschoff, 'names are records, living personal memories of persons and events. From the natural standpoint, there are more names, more passion, more tragedy and more comedy, more humanity and inhumanity than is possible for some civilised people to realise'.[1]

Igbo names therefore constitute invaluable archives in which traditional Igbo wisdom and beliefs are enshrined. What then, do we learn from the Igbo personal names for God?

The Igbo have three personal names for God: *Chukwu*, the Great Chi;[2] *Chineke*, Chi the Creator; *Osebuluwa* or *Olisa* (shortened form), Carrier of the world. Although all three names are now used throughout Igboland, each one stems from a different area. Thus, according to Basden:

Several names are appropriated to the Supreme Being which, more or less, assimilated the underlying ideas of some particular

attributes. In the southern parts of the country, He is known as
Chineke (God, the Creator).

In the northern parts, the term *Chukwu* (*Chukwu* – the great God)
is the more common title. In some districts He is spoken of as
Olisa-bulu-uwa or, in one word, *Olisa*. This conveys the meaning of
the 'god who fashions the world'.[3]

A detailed study of these three personal names and other
title-names given to God throws a great deal of light on the
Igbo concept of Him.

Igbo names for God

The definition of Chi

The first two names, *Chukwu* and *Chineke,* are both composed of two words. *Chukwu* is composed of *Chi* and *Ukwu,*
while *Chineke* is composed of *Chi* and *Eke*. From this it
appears that the important word in both cases is *Chi*. What
does *Chi* mean? *Chi*, in my view, is one of those archaic root
words which are found in some languages and which defy
all etymology. Different authors have suggested different
meanings. Talbot, for example, thinks that *Chi* is the
original name for the 'Supreme Being'. According to him:
'The old word seems to have been *Chi*, sometimes called
Chi-Ukwu, the Great Chi, the attribute was applied by most
Ibo, as in the *Chukwu Oke Abiama* . . . to distinguish it from
the personal *Chi*.'[4] *Chi* therefore, in his view, is the personal
name for God and needs no translation. Many other
authorities however, like Basden and Meek, disagree with
him.

Basden thinks that *chi* seems almost to be a generic word
for 'god' (in small letters). With a qualifying attribute, it
becomes or denotes a distinctive god, hence we have *Chi*
used in conjunction with *Ukwu*, giving *Chi-Ukwu*, the Great
God.[5] Meek translates *Chi* as 'spirit'. He describes God as the
over-soul analogous to *Chi* – the accompanying soul which
he sends into each person. He writes: 'One of the most
striking doctrines of the Ibo is that every human being has
associated with his personality, a genius or spiritual double

known as *Chi*.[6] He then goes on to compare this conception of a transcendent self to the Egyptian notion of *Ka*, which was the double or genius of a man, an ancestral emanation, apparently, which guided and protected him during his lifetime and to which he returned after death.

It is therefore no surprise that the word and concept of *Chi* has continued to intrigue many foreign writers because although it is a fundamental word in the Igbo religious system, it is at the same time so difficult to grasp. This is perhaps a case where only the Igbo, who has lived his religion, whose language, culture and modes of thought and expression are all permeated by it, can best explain the terminology and the meanings it implies. All the above writers are right up to a point; at the same time, none of them is exactly right. What each has seen and described of *Chi* is like the blind men who went to experience an elephant. Each described a part of the elephant, and even when all their descriptions were put together, we were not given any true idea of what an elephant was like.

The word *Chi* used in a religious context, evokes three related concepts namely: the 'Supreme Being', the 'Guardian Spirit', and the idea of 'Destiny' or 'Fortune'. Only the context can show which of the three is uppermost in an Igbo's mind when he uses the word *Chi*. This is borne out by the fact that the word appears in many Igbo proverbs, sometimes referring to one concept, sometimes to another: the Supreme Being, one's personal spirit-guardian, or even one's destiny.

1 *Chi as Supreme Being:*

Chi ma onye ọga enye ma onye ọga enye amaghi	God knows to whom he will give, but who will receive does not know.
Okike kere onye bụ Chi ya	One's Creator is his God.
Ehi n'enweghi odụ, Chi ya n'achụrụ ya ijiji	God drives away flies for a cow which has no tail.
Chi adaghi anụ ihe ọzọ sọsọ atụgh na amughi.	God does not hear any other thing except prayers to conceive and give birth.

2 *Chi as personal spirit-guardian:*

Ebe onye dara ka Chi ya kwaturu ya	Where a person falls it is his personal spirit-guardian who pushed him down.
Ọka madụ ka Chi ya	If you are stronger than a person, you are also stronger than his personal spirit-guardian.
Ofu nne na amụ, ma ofu Chi adaghi eke	Two people can have the same mother, but they cannot have identical personal spirit-guardians.

3 *Chi as Destiny:*

Agbataghi Ajọ Chi n' ụzọ ọlụ	You cannot escape bad fortune by resourcefulness
Chi jiere onye chi ọjọọ ọnagh abọ abọ	When darkness falls for an unfortunate man, it is endless.
Onye Ajo Chi kpatara nkụ ewu taa ya	A goat eats even the firewood of an unfortunate man.

Admittedly, it is not always easy to distinguish which of the three concepts is intended. This apparent confusion stems from the Igbo belief that when God creates each person, He gives him a *Chi* – a guardian spirit. God is believed to give the *Chi* a choice between two parcels of fortune, one better than the other. Whichever the *Chi* chooses contains the total luck in the destiny which the child entrusted to his care will have. This fortune in itself is also referred to as *chi*. Thus, a lucky man is called *onye chi ọma*, 'someone who has a good *chi*', and an unfortunate man is called *onye chi ọjọọ*, 'someone who has a bad *chi*'.

In effect, we have a highly confusing situation where the same word applies to God, to the spirit-guardian, and to the fortune of each person. Which of these has the greater claim? Which gives us the best clue to the meaning of this important word?

The idea of Destiny so pervades Igbo life and thought that it is reasonable to assume that it is an ancient and basic concept in the Igbo system of belief. Every event in a man's life whether it be success or failure is *ọnatara chi*, a gift of destiny. The goal of a man's life is to achieve his *akara aka* or *Akara chi* – the destiny imprinted on his palm. It would therefore seem that *chi* primarily suggests the idea of destiny in the mind of the Igbo. If one must talk of the transposition of words in this context, one would say that the word *chi* applies primarily to destiny and secondarily to the spirit-guardian. In fact, the spirit-guardian *Chi* is but the personification of individual destiny *Chi*. So the suggestion of translating *Chi* merely as 'spirit' or as a generic word for 'god', errs by defect. *Chi* is indeed a spirit, but a special kind of spirit, precisely the spirit associated with a person's destiny and which directs its realization.

The meaning of Chukwu

The simple, literal meaning of *Chukwu* is the 'Great Chi'. If the above interpretation of *Chi* is accepted, *Chukwu* would become the 'Great Controller of destiny' of the universe (or the Divine Providence). One might almost draw the parallel that *Chukwu* is to the universe in the same way as *Chi* is to the controller of individual destiny. The best rendering of *Chukwu*, in my view, would therefore be the 'Great Providence'.[7]

The meaning of Chineke

Now we come to *Chineke*. Traditionally, this name was more commonly used in the southern parts of Igboland: Owerri, Umuahia, Okigwe and the Delta areas, in preference to *Chukwu*. Now it has spread throughout Igboland and has been further popularized by its use in translating 'God' in the Bible. This has led many to believe that it was introduced by the missionaries, but this is not so – as we shall see.

Chineke, like *Chukwu*, is composed of two words: *Chi* and *Eke*. *Chi* as we now understand it means 'providence'. What does *Eke* mean?

Eke, like *Chi*, is a victim of the paucity of Igbo vocabulary. It can be used to translate up to seven different things – snake, market-day, create, divine, tie, a spirit, and a share –

depending on how it is pronounced and the context in which it is used.[8] When used to denote the Supreme Being, it unmistakably refers to the verb *ike*, to create. According to Anozia 'the verb "to create" in Igbo is never used of any other activity, not even metaphorically'.[9]

However, there is a creative emanation of God called *Eke*. Although *Eke* is intimately connected with creative action, he does not create. Igbo belief has it, that when *Chukwu* creates, *Chi* chooses the destiny of the creature, and *Eke* (or *Okike*) lets him out into the world. Igbo belief highly esteems the rôle of *Eke*, but an Igbo proverb assures us that *Eke, kelu onye bu Chi ya*, 'you may talk of a person's *Eke* but his creator is God'. *Chineke* therefore means 'Chi who creates', i.e. Creator Providence or a Provident Creator. God's creative act is a continuing one, for He continues to sustain and provide for his creatures.

The meaning of Osebuluwa

God can also be called *Osebuluwa* or its abbreviated form, *Olisa*. The contracted form resembles the names for the Supreme Being usèd by the Benin and their related tribes: the Edo (*Osanowa*), the Sobo (*Orisha Neburuwa*), the Esa and Kukuruku (*Oselebua*). As these and the western Igbo were for a long time part of the Benin empire, one might reasonably conclude that the name could have derived from the same source as the Benin *Osanowa*.[10] The Igbo abbreviated form *Olisa* sounds very like the Yoruba *Orisha*.

The interpretations Basden and Anozia gave to this name are in my view inexact. According to Basden, *Olisabuluwa* 'conveys the meaning of the "god who fashions the world" '.[11] It must be said, however, that no idea of fashioning, *ime*, or creating, *ike,* is contained in this name. While Basden's translation does not bring out the idea of 'carrying the world', *bulu uwa*, Dr. Anozia is convinced that *Olisa* 'is not an original Igbo word', but is borrowed from the Yoruba among whom it means 'the source and sustainer of the world'.[12] There is no proof that the Igbo word *Olisa* was borrowed from the Yoruba any more than the Yoruba word was borrowed from the Igbo. *Olisa* or its dialectal version *Orisa* is in fact an Igbo word, very often used in the sense of 'transcend' or 'permeate', 'take complete possession of', 'completely eat up'. For example the Igbo say, *Oligo ya aru*, 'it has eaten up his body' or *oligo ya mme*, 'it has eaten up his blood'; both mean that it has become a part of him. *Olisa* would therefore literally mean 'He who is spread out everywhere', or 'He who permeates everything', i.e. the Transcendent One, the Immense. This interpretation of its meaning is confirmed by the meaning of the name in its full form, *Olisa N'obuluwa*, 'he who is spread out everywhere and carrying the world' i.e. the immense, and sustainer of the world. Fr. Emenceta's view is somewhat different. According to him, *Olisa* means 'container of the universe', and *buluwa* means 'one who permeates the world'.[13]

The idea of carrying the world must not be understood in the literal and physical sense. God is not conceived like the god Atlas. He is carrying the world because His continuing power to sustain it is necessary to keep the world going. He continues to provide for it. He is therefore the Great Providence that continues to keep and guide the world. An ancient and popular Igbo song celebrates this belief:

Oyoyo uwa di ya	Beauty! The (world) is full of enjoyment
Oyoyo uwa di ya	Beauty! There is joy in the world
Chukwu sel'aka	But should God remove his hand
Uwa agwu	The world would vanish.[14]

Other title-names for God

Besides the three personal names already analysed, the Igbo give God many other names. These are sometimes local variations on the personal names; more often, they are title-names or praise-names of God. Among the Igbo a man's social importance can often be gauged by his title-names, or *Aha Otutu*. These also reflect a person's character or achievements, his rank, office or even philosophy of life.[15] For example, in a parish where I once worked, my own *Aha Otutu* was *Eze olelu n'iru ya*, 'King during whose reign aspirations are realized'. This was because the parishioners' long-held hope of building a parish church was realized while I was there. An elder in the same community took for himself this highly philosophical title-name, *Okpa Kwụlọtọ*: 'When a leg is standing it belongs to the community; when it falls, it belongs to its owner.' This means that the community demands your services when you are in good health; when you are sick, you look after yourself.

A very common and ancient title-name hails God as *Chukwu Abiama*, 'The Great Providence of the universe'.[16] Chukwu is not a tribal deity. This is of great significance because most Igbo deities have no influence outside the village which 'owns' them. So it is usual when naming a deity to name the group which owns it, like *Idemili Obosi*, *Ụlasi* of Ọkija, *Omaliko Abatete*, *Igwe-kala* of Umunnọha etc. *Chukwu*'s sovereignty cuts across all tribal boundaries; He owns and rules the whole world.

Other names hail him as *Agbala-ji-igwe*, 'the great pillar holding up the heavens'; *Chi-di-n'enu*, 'the spirit that lives above'; *Chi Okike*, 'the Creator Providence'.[17] He is *Ezechitoke* – King Providence, the Creator; *Olisa bi n'enu*, 'the Immense One living above'; *Igwe ka Ala*, 'Heaven greater than the earth'. This association of God with the sky or heaven is found in many other title-names: God is *Obasi di n'enu*, 'the Lord above'.[18] More often He is simply called *Enu*, 'Heaven', as in the question *Enu nụrụkwọ*, 'Heaven, have you heard?' In some places he is called *Chinụwa*, 'the Lord owner of the world'.

Still more interesting are the names which address God as *Otu aka oru mba*, 'He who can destroy twenty towns with a wave of the hand'; *Onye ana ekpere*, 'He whom all beseech'; *Onye okwu biri na ọnụ ya*, 'final arbiter';[19] *Eze bi n'igwe ọgọdọ ya n'akpụ N'ala*, 'the King who lives in the sky and his clothes touch and roll on the ground'. Some title-names attempt to convey the essence of God. God is often called *Ama-Ama-Amasi-Amasi*, 'One known but never comprehended'. He is often referred to as *Anya Ozighololo*, 'the all-seeing eye, the eye that penetrates all creation, and sees even the unspoken thought'. Another title-name which expresses the frustration of the Igbo at their failure to comprehend the incomprehensible, calls God *Ejeruo*, the *terminus ad quem*, beyond which one cannot proceed any further.[20]

Other title-names curiously associated God with the sun, *Anyanwu*. In the Awka region, a common title-name for God is *Anyanwu na Agbala*. *Anyanwu* literally means the sun; *Agbala* means a powerful being, yet it would be inaccurate to translate this name as 'the Powerful Being living in the sun'. Some informants tell me that *Anyanwu na Agbala* is a composite being standing for God, and for his son, *Agbala*. This is borne out by the term *Agbala Chukwu Okike*, 'Agbala, son of God the Creator', which is often used to designate *Agbala* alone.[21] Another such name which seems to identify God with the sun is *Anyanwu na Eze enu*; which literally means 'the sun and king of the sky'. This name is very widely used in Igboland. One of the sacrifices which are offered directly to God is made under this name: *Ilu onu Anyanwu na Eze-enu* or *Ilu onu Anyanwu na Agbala*, 'pitching the altar of God'.

The imagery contained in the African names for God

'The Akan doctrine of God,' writes Danquah, 'is the doctrine of an Akan type of God.' He explains thus: 'The true God is not of several kinds, but He can be known under several degrees or colours, for each people has a name for God, and in the name is to be found (the) quality or colour in God which most appeals to their racial mind.'[22] The Igbo personal names and title-names for God recorded above provide us with a wealth of data as to how the Igbo think of Him. How do they compare with those of other African peoples?

Mgr. Le Roy and Professor E. Damman have each independently carried out extensive studies of the imagery and ideas woven into the African personal names for God. Le Roy noted that most of the Africans he studied employed terms which include imagery such as life, breath, heart, shadow, all of which are closely connected with the human person to designate man, or even the dead. To designate the non-human spirits, they draw their images from elements which are strange to man such as air and wind, but to give God a name they adopt a very curious procedure. Instead of trying to coin words to represent the incomprehensible nature of God, they prefer to name Him by epithet – an attribute, or quality – and add that this quality belongs to Him in a supreme degree.

Sometimes God is named through a symbol which indicates His habitat. His power or His greatness. Some names of God represent Him principally as the Maker, Organizer and Creator of the world, for example *Mumba* of the Swahili and their related tribes, *Katonda* of the Ganda, *Nyambi* of Lozi, *Nzambi* of the Luango and *Nzaine* of the Fan of Gabon all refer to God as Creator. Other creative rôles emphasize His power and greatness: *Mwiny'ezi*, 'the powerful', similarly, *Nzulu* of the Zulu means 'The Great Great', *Mulofo* of the Luba means the Chief or Lord. Still others call God the 'Great Spirit of the universe', *Molimo*. Finally, certain names refer to God as 'He who is above', *Mulungu*, or *Muango*, 'the One of the light or the sun', thus naming God through his supposed habitat.[23]

Damman tried to show that many African names for God refer to his supposed habitat – the sky, the sun, rain, rainbow, or the place of the dead. He concludes, 'Though only a small number of African languages have been examined for their designation of their High God, two prevailing conceptions have been ascertained: on the one hand, the connexion with the sky and its phenomena and with the celestial bodies and, on the other, with the realm of the dead and the ancestors'.[24] He also suggests as characteristic an apotheosis whereby a god formerly located in the underworld is promoted to sky-God.

From the observations of Le Roy and Damman, it would seem that the images emphasized by African personal names for God can be put into four categories:

Images	Names	Tribe
A *The Maker or Creator*	Mu'umba	Swahili
(*of the world*)	Mbumba	Loango
	Karunga	Herero
	Katonda	Ganda
	Chineke	Igbo
B *The Most Powerful (Spirit),*	Olodumare	Yoruba
the greatest, the perfect	Nkulu-Nkulu	Zulu
one	Chukwu	Igbo
	Leza	Bemba
	Mulofo	Luba
	Leza	Tonga

C *The Spirit of the Universe*	Mwinyezi	Swahili (tube)
	Onyankupon	Akan
	Molimo	Bantu
	Kwot	Nuer
	Osebuluwa	Igbo
D *God is named after his*	Onyame	Akan
Habitat (Sky or Sun)	Chido	Jukun
	Olorun	Yoruba
	Etonde	Chaga
	Soko	Nupe
	Ngewo	Mende
	Nhialic	Dinka
	Chiuta	Chewa
	Aondo	Tiv

It would seem that the African names for God are fairly evenly distributed among the four classifications, but a greater proportion refer to the sky and its phenomena — sun, rain, rainbow.

In fact, it has been reported of many African tribes that the same names denote both the Supreme Being and the firmament itself, the sky, or even rain. So one may say indifferently 'It is raining' or 'God is falling'; 'Dawn is breaking' or 'God is dawning'. The name for God among the Tiv of Nigeria is *Aondo*, but the Tiv may also say *Aondokume*, 'Aondo roars' when it thunders or *Aondo nyir*, 'Aondo is falling' when it is raining.[25]

Whatever the explanation, a note of caution must be sounded about etymological and philological approaches to the study of African religious beliefs, especially for those who discuss languages which are not their mother tongue. As I have already mentioned, because of the paucity of vocabulary in some African languages, the same word sometimes carries several meanings. It therefore might be wrong to conclude that because the same word is used for God and the sun that the group using it are Sun worshippers, or that the sun or the sky is the Supreme Being. This is well illustrated by the Igbo word *Chi*, the root word in two of the Igbo names for God: *Chukwu* and *Chineke*. But the Igbo also say *chi ejeila*, 'it is dusk' and *chi efola*, 'it is dawn'. *Chi* in this case means daylight, but there is not the slightest connection in the mind of the Igbo between God and daylight.

Whether the two uses of the identically spelt word were ever connected in the remote and misty past can only be conjecture.[26]

The meanings of some of the names show that our classification is not airtight. Some names combine two or more images. The name *Chauta*, 'the Great One of the Bow', seems to combine the B and D images – the idea of the Great Spirit and a sky phenomenon. *Chukwu* combines C and B, while *Chineke* combines A and C. The third name *Osebuluwa* if translated as 'the Immense Sustainer of the world', could be said to combine categories A, B and C. Curiously, none of the three Igbo names makes any reference to the sun.

A variety of the imagery used in the Igbo names and title-names of God draws directly from Igbo experience. We can draw the conclusion that the prefix *Chi* evokes the Igbo belief that each person's *Chi* receives his destiny from God, who is *Chukwu* – the Great *Chi*. *Chineke* reminds us that creation is an essential attribute of God. Another essential – the continuing sustenance of the world by God – is well portrayed in the names *Osebuluwa* and *Agbala-ji-igwe*, 'the powerful and kindly being who is carrying the world'. From the interpretation of the imagery employed in these names, one is already in a position to draw up a list of His attributes.

Notes

1 Wieschoff, W. A. 'Social significance of names among the Ibos of Nigeria' in *American Anthropologist*, 43 (1941) pp.212–22.
2 This word, pronounced like 'chi' in 'children' has been variously written *Chi, Ci, Tsi*. In this book, we shall retain the more common forms *Chi* and *Chukwu*.
3 Basden, G. T. *Niger Ibos* (London, 1966) p.37.
4 Talbot, P. A. *The Peoples of Southern Nigeria* (London, 1926).
5 Basden, G. T. op. cit. (1966) p.37.
6 Meek, C. K. *Law and Authority in a Nigerian Tribe* (London, 1937) p.20.
7 Williams, J. J. *Africa's God* (1938) p.209 quoting a reply

to a questionnaire received from (the late) Rev.Fr. Paul Emecheta, the first Igbo priest.

8 Another typical example is the Igbo word 'Akwa' which could mean egg, tears, sew, bridge, cloth, funeral, push, packing etc.

9 Anozia, I. P. unpublished thesis, 'The Religious Import of Igbo Names', Urban University, Rome (1968) p.39.

10 Talbot, P. A. *The Peoples of Southern Nigeria* (London, 1926) Vol. II, p.41.

11 Basden, G. T. op. cit. (1966) p.37.

12 Anozia, I. P. op. cit. (1968) p.39.

13 Williams, J. J. op. cit. (1930) p.210.

14 Anozia, I. P. op. cit. (1968) p.40 (the translation is mine).

15 Arinze, F. A. *Sacrifice in Ibo Religion* (Ibadan, 1970) p.9.

16 This name features more in ancient ritual prayers. Crowther, S. and Taylor, J. *The Gospel on the Banks of the Niger* (1968 ed.) p.348.

17 Horton, W. R. C. 'God, man, and the land in a Northern Ibo Village-Group', *Africa*, 26 (Jan. 1956) p.12.

18 Uchendu, V. C. *The Igbo of Southeast Nigeria* (1965) p.95.

19 Ekejiuba, F. 'Aro World View', *West African Religion* (1970).

20 Obi, C. 'Igbo Marriage and Christianity', unpublished thesis, Urban University, Rome (1970) p.23.

21 Tape-recorded interview with the Ezeana of Awka (4th May, 1972).

22 Danquah, J. B. *Akan Doctrine of God* (London, 1944) p.45.

23 Le Roy, Mgr. *Les Religions des Primitifs* (Paris, 1906) p.172.

24 Damman, E. 'A tentative philological Typology of some African High Deities', *Journal of Religion in Africa*, II (1970) p.6.

25 Downes, R. M. *Tiv Religion* (Ibadan, 1971) p.17.

26 Basden, G. T. op. cit. (1966) p.47.

3   The attributes of God

While analysing the ideas about God contained in myths and the names and title-names for God, we came across several of His attributes. These included His providence, His omnipotence, His transcendence, His immanence, His immensity, and so forth. More information can be gathered from a study of Igbo proverbs, sayings, songs, and expressions used in everyday life. Of special interest are the hundreds of theophoric names (i.e. names composed of God's attributes) which the Igbo give to their children.[1] From these names alone, one can construct a whole treatise on Igbo theodicy. These names are not the result of Christian influence. Pagans have used them from time immemorial.[2] A colleague of mine wrote a thesis entitled *The Religious Import of Igbo Names* in which he studied and analysed the doctrinal content of ninety-three such theophoric names under twelve headings representing the nature and attributes of God, and His relation to man.[3] Here we shall look at a selection of those attributes which feature most often in Igbo expressions, daily life, and worship.

God as Creator

The creative rôle of God is abundantly illustrated in the cosmogonic myths analysed in chapter 1. To summarize: Chukwu is a creator. Creating is his prerogative; no other being can create. In fact, every other being is created. This is very clear in the Igbo mind. Igbo myths presume that God pre-existed the world and everything else that is known to exist. Making this presumption then, the myths then go on to explain the existence of every other thing by means of special and direct interventions by Chukwu, who is an uncaused cause, an uncreated creator.

The Igbo have many names for God which acclaim his rôle as creator of the universe. As well as Chineke, the Provident Creator, he is also called *Chi Okike*, 'the Creator'; *Eze Chito-Oke*, 'King, Providence, Creator'; *Ihe Kere uwa* 'Creator of the world'; *Oke kere uwa*, 'Creator, maker of the world'; *Oke kere mmadu*, 'Creator who created mankind'. God's creation of mankind is not limited merely to bringing man into existence or giving him life. The Igbo believe that each and every faculty and talent of each and every person is given to him by God. Hence you find such expressions as *Chukwu kere ye, kegburu ya 'ekegbu'*, 'The God who created him, very poorly endowed him', or *Chukwu nyere ya ezigbo uche*, 'God gave him great common sense'.

Furthermore, God is still creating, every minute of every day, and the Igbo believe that every person's *Chi* is directly created by God at the very instant of his conception. Hence the Igbo proverbs: *Ofu nne na amu ma ofu chi adighi eke*, 'You may indeed come from the same mother, but you have different gifts from God', or *Okike kere onye bu chi ya* – 'One's creator is his God'.

Many of the Igbo theophoric names emphasize God's eminent rôle as Creator of the world and of each individual:

Chukwukere God-created

This name recognizes the special intervention of God in the circumstances surrounding the birth of the child. It reasserts in a spirit of faith and with thanksgiving a fact which is evident to every Igbo. God is indeed the creator of this child.

Nwachukwu Nyere God-given child

In the minds of parents who give this name is the thought: 'It could not be explained otherwise; this child is a gesture of the kindness and mercy of God towards us.'

Okechukwu God's gift

Or God's creature.

Madueke Not created by man

Or simply, 'Man does not create'. This name may be given to children who have poor health or are deformed. By using this name, the parents reaffirm their faith and confidence that God who made him can still make him survive, or help him overcome his disabilities by giving him other talents.

Onyeneke Who creates?

A fundamental question, but the answer is clear as daylight itself to every Igbo: God is the Creator.

The Unicity of God

For the Igbo, Chukwu is one and can only be one. *Chukwu abụọ*, two Gods, or *Chukwu ga*, many Gods, cannot be imagined, it is an absurdity. The phrase 'Two Gods' is a contradiction in terms. Some writers perhaps do not appreciate how jarring it could be to the ear of an Igbo to refer to the deities or the *Arụsi*, nature spirits, as gods. Understandably, the claim of God's unicity becomes very perplexing when one considers the large numbers of these *Arụsi*, and that some of them have certain divine attributes and are worshipped. But this presents no difficulty to the Igbo. Judeo-Christian traditions have developed a dialectic between monotheism and polytheism which is completely foreign to African traditional religion. The belief in one God and many deities is not contradictory but complementary. In fact, the unicity of God is enhanced rather than compromised by belief in deities who are not gods, nor are they equal to God. They differ from God not only in their power and excellence, but by their very nature. God is essentially the uncreated Creator of everything. There cannot be two such beings.

This is borne out by the fact that there are hardly any two Igbo communities which worship identical sets of deities and *Arụsi*. The liturgical calendar of each village-group has a different set of divinities, yet every Igbo group worships Chukwu as Creator and Lord of the whole world. Even more interesting is the fact that although the deities of the other tribes are considered hostile and dangerous, the Igbo have recognized the Supreme Being of neighbouring tribes as identical with Chukwu and have adopted their names as alternative names for Him. From the neighbouring Edo they probably adopted the name *Osebuluwa*. The Edo name for God is *Osanobuwa*. From the Efiks to their south-east, the Igbo have adopted and freely use the term *Obassi*. Chukwu is sometimes greeted as *Obassi di n'elu*. Hence God is not supreme among the gods in the henotheistic sense. He is not just the Supreme God of the Igbo, he is the same as the *Osanobuwa* of the Bini, the *Obassi* of the Efik, the *Tamuno* of Kalabari, the *Olodumare* of the Yoruba, the *Suku* of the Jukun.

Some Igbo proverbs confirm the unicity of God, while many others make very cynical references to the divinities. One may sometimes question whether the cult of the divinities can really be called worship as it is based on the principle of strict reciprocity with very little affection or devotion. For example, an Igbo proverb says, *Aga aghapuru umu mmo nri gbawara ha na nkita ogu*, 'Shall I offer food to the spirits and prevent dogs from eating them?' Another says, *Aga na achu aja ha ikpe na ama ndi mmuo*, 'We shall continue to fulfil our duty to offer sacrifices so that the fault will be that of the spirits'. But Chukwu is *Onye okwu biri na onu ya*, 'God is the final arbiter'. Yes, *dibia*, the diviner, can manipulate the deities, but he cannot manipulate God. Hence the Igbo name *Chukwuka-Dibia*, 'God is greater than any medicine-man'.

The Igbo personal names for God emphasize the unicity of God. The name Chukwu – the Great Providence – establishes the pre-eminence of God over the deities. God is called Chukwu Abiama, 'the Great Providence of the whole universe'. He is above all.

God is Omnipotent

Chukwu is omnipotent. His power is seen in His great work of creation. The wonders of the world tell of His greatness. The sun, the moon, the seasons, the immense sky – all are the work of His hands and are dependent on Him. Hence His most common and most appropriate personal name among the Igbo is Chukwu, the Great Providence. The Earth-deity is great; in fact she is the most beloved, the most revered and certainly the most feared deity among the Igbo. Still, Chukwu is sometimes addressed as *Igwekala*, 'Heaven greater than the earth'. The immensity of the sky fascinates the Igbo. The sky itself, *Igwe*, is a powerful deity but Chukwu is the *Agbala ji Igwe*, 'the great pillar holding up the sky'. His other similar name *Osebuluwa* shows not only that God is greater than the world, but also that the world with all its power and wonders is dependent on God for its very existence. The Igbo song quoted in the previous chapter says, '*Chukwu sel'aka ụwa agwụ*', 'If God removes his hands, the world will end'. The ancient name Chukwu Abiama – Lord God of the universe — confirms this supremacy of God over the universe.

The Igbo do not see God's greatness and omnipotence only in relation to the material world; they also see it in His relation to the spiritual world. Other spirits may sometimes be referred to as *Chi* – spirit protector. A village or a town may have its *Chi*, but only God is *Chi-Ukwu*, the great Chi, Lord of the Universe. *Chukwu Kere ihe nile*, 'God created everything'. The subordination of the spirits to God is sometimes expressed in terms of a father/son relationship, or a master/servant relationship. The spirits are sometimes called sons of God, or His messengers.

God is greater than man. The Igbo say *Chukwu ji ndụ*, 'Life is in the hand of God'; *Ihe nile di Chukwu na aka*, 'Everything is in the hand of God'.

Many Igbo personal names tell of God's omnipotence and His greatness; some state the simple fact that God is omnipotent, others compare His power to the power of other powerful beings and affirm that God's power far exceeds theirs. For example:

Chukwu-wu-ike God is power

This name expresses God's omnipotence very forcefully, yet in an abstract way. The Igbo word *wụ* (or *bụ*) is a verb of identification. It is therefore stronger than its English rendering 'is'. *Ike* means power, energy, force, strength. A more exact translation may be 'God is power itself'.

Onyeka Chukwu Who is greater than God?

This name puts the fact of God's omnipotence in a negative and interrogative form. The form is confident, however, in as much as it challenges whoever has a contrary view to say so. Needless to say, it is an axiom among the Igbo that *Onwegh onye ka Chukwu*, 'Nobody is greater than God'.

Chukwu ebuka God is very great

The Igbo language cannot stretch itself to a more superlative degree.

Chukwu ka   God is the greatest

This may also be understood as 'God is transcendent'.

Chukwu nweike   God is the owner of strength

This name is a warning to men that their strength or power, whether based on wealth, authority or physical strength, is a gift from God.

Ifeanyi Chukwu   Nothing is impossible for God

This is a very picturesque name, and affirms God's omnipotence with typical Igbo imagery. *Inyi alo* means 'to be heavy', specifically the type of weight one feels when one carries something on the head in the traditional Igbo way. A very heavy load would force one down. So an impossible task is *ife nyilụ dike* – what has forced down a powerful man i.e. what is beyond him. This name states that with God no such thing exists – there is nothing beyond God.

Chikwuka dibia   God is more powerful than the medicine man

The Igbo consult the *dibia*, medicine-man, in all of life's crises, but they know that when God decrees, the *dibia*'s divination and herbs are of no avail. The Igbo proverb states this succinctly: *Chukwu bie okwu, ile dibia abụrụ eziokwu*, 'when God settles an issue, the *dibia*'s tongue begins to tell the truth'.

God is Transcendent

Chukwu is not only omnipotent but also transcendent. He is not only distinct from the world or any other creature but infinitely excels over them in power and excellence. No limit can be put to his power and excellence by any human mind or imagination.

The transcendence of God in relation to the universe is already implied in some of his personal and title-names. *Osebuluwa* – Lord carrier of the world – is a metaphorical way of stating that God far surpasses the world. He is called *Ezechitoke* 'King, Lord, and Creator'. He is *Eze Enu* – 'King of the Heavens', but he is also *Eze bi n'igwe, ọgọdọ ya na-a kpụ n'ala*, 'King who lives in the sky and his clothes touch and roll over the ground'. His transcendence and his immanence, thus expressed, seem to be contradictory although they are really complementary. Though some writers on African traditional religion try to emphasize God's transcendence at the expense of his immanence by talking of a 'withdrawn God' or of the 'withdrawal of Africa's God', this Igbo name demonstrates an admirable blend of these two essential but apparently paradoxical attributes. God is far above in the heavens in kingly majesty and exaltation, but yet he fills the whole earth with his presence – his enormous loin cloth falls and covers the earth.

Chukwu is *Anya-Ozighololo*, 'the eye that sees through and through'. This metaphorical expression is certainly drawn from the sun which is also called a 'big eye', *Anya-Nwu*. The sun is an eye whose light reaches every part of the world, but more than the sun, God is described as an eye which pierces through and sees into everything. This is the force of the term *Ozighololo,* which is onomatopoeic, apparently reproducing the sound of water being poured into a deep hole, which indicates that it is open and very deep.

Chukwu also transcends the human mind. Hence He is called *Ama-ama-Amasi-Amasi*, 'Being which is known but cannot be fully known'. God is thus incomprehensible. Chukwu is also called *Ejelue*, 'that beyond which it is impossible to go'. God's transcendence is also celebrated in some theophoric names:

Olisanumba God does not hear reproaches

Nobody can be so naive as to scold God. Such a one would be kicking against the goad – God does not even hear it; we are so insignificant before Him.

Chukwubisi God is first, God is the head

This is the Igbo way of saying that God is Alpha – beginning of all beginnings.

Onyedika chukwu Who is like God? Who can be likened to God?

The answer is, of course, nobody. He is infinitely above all men.

God is King

Another favourite image used to express the transcendence of God is the image of kingship. Kingship is not a characteristic institution in Igbo societies: *Igbo enwe eze*, 'Igbo have no kings'. But they certainly know how exalted kingly dignity is. Some Igbo societies along the banks of the Niger have adopted kingly systems through long contact with the ancient and famous Benin empire. The majesty, power and dignity of *Eze Idu na Oba*, Oba of Benin, are celebrated in many an ancient Igbo folktale. But the egalitarian Igbo have another traditional concept of kingship. They say, *Onye ọbula wụ eze na obi be nna ya*, 'Everybody is king in his father's estate'. The title *Eze* or 'king' is given to anybody who has attained an extraordinary degree of success in any field. Thus an exceptionally successful yam farmer is called *Eze ji*, king of yams. A good orator is called *Ezeokwu*, king of speech – or master speaker.

For the Igbo, God is king both in the sense of ruler, and in the sense of possessor of infinitely excellent qualities. Igbo proverbs say *Chi bu eze* 'God is king'. We have already noted that God is called *Eze Enu* – King above. In fact, the only sacrifice known in Igbo religion to be offered directly to God is called *Ilụ Anyanwụ na Eze Enu*, 'Sacrifice to the king of the sky'. God is King of kings, hence the saying *Chukwu nwe eze* – 'God owns the king'.

God's Providence

The concept of divine providence is one which has great appeal for the Igbo mind. The Igbo primarily conceives of God as the great Lord Creator who continues to sustain, guard and cater for the needs of the world. God did not abandon the world after its creation. Even the material universe is in the hands of God and needs his continuous sustenance. Remember that the Igbo song says, *Chukwu selụ aka ụwa agwu*, 'If God removes his hands the world will end'. Another Igbo song asks, *Ụwa bụdụ nke onye?*, 'to whom does the world belong?' The answer is known to every Igbo: *Ihe nile di n'aka Chukwu* 'Everything is in the hands of God'. *Chi nwe ụwa*, 'God owns the world', is a major article in the Igbo creed. Some Igbo even have *Chinụwa*, God – owner of the world, as one of God's personal names.

God's providential care for men and for the other creatures in the world is a characteristic feature of the Igbo world-view. God personally sustains and rules the universe, hence he is *Chi oke Abiama*, 'creator, guide and ruler of the world'. He also directs the destinies of all other creatures through parts or emanations of himself called *Chi*, which he gives to each and every individual. Every plant, animal, or man has a personal Chi which, like a guardian angel, directs his affairs. God, however, is the great Chi who may at his discretion interfere directly and personally in the affairs of every single individual, or thing. He determines each person's birth and death, hence the Igbo proverb: *Chi adaghi anụ ihe ọzọ na abụghi atụgh na amụgh*, 'God is bored with petitions to conceive and to give birth'. *Chi onye adigh n'izu, ọnwụ agaghi egbu ya*, 'Without God's consent, death cannot kill'.

God sometimes makes and unmakes kings. *Chi kpụrụ nwaeze ekwela nwaeze rụo ntụ* 'May God who made the king, not let him lose glory'. God helps and protects the helpless – *Ehi n'enweghi ọdụ, Chi ya n'achụrụ ya ijiji*, 'God drives away flies for a cow which has no tail'.

The Igbo belief in divine providence sometimes seems to reach fatalistic proportions: *Onye Chi ya kwetara ofufu ọbagodu ubi be ya ọga efuriri*, 'If your Chi has destined that you will get lost, you can even get lost in your garden'. *Agbataghi Ajọ Chi n'ụzọ oru*, 'you cannot change your unfortunate lot by being industrious'. Yet paradoxically far from being fatalistic in practical life, the Igbo are a very industrious and most resourceful people; they believe that *Onye kwe, Chi ya ekwe*, 'if a man is determined, his Chi will support him'. This is the African version of the proverb, 'God helps those who help themselves'.

Most Igbo theophoric names are fruit of men's experience of Divine Providence. There are those which attribute particular effects or experiences of life to God's direct intervention, while others show resignation to the will and plan of God.

Izuchukwu The plan of God

In fact, this is an abbreviation of a popular saying *Ife Chukwu zubelu ga eme*, 'Whatever God has planned must happen'. Another version of the name is **Chizube**, God has planned (wealth, prosperity, etc. for me.)

Uzochukwu The way of God

The full expression should be *Uzọ Chukwu ka mma* God's way (plan) is the best.

Arinze Chukwu Thanks to God's intervention

This name is very frequently used as an exclamation. It is the Igbo equivalent of 'Thanks be to God!'.

Okechukwu This is the share allotted to me by God, my God-given lot

Okwosa The verdict of providence

Names such as these which praise God's providential concern for man can be counted in their hundreds. This confirms my earlier statement that God is primarily and fundamentally conceived as the Great Providence, guiding the universe and especially men.

God is All-knowing

The Igbo are strong in their belief that God knows everything. Certain Igbo expressions indicate that God knows the most hidden secrets, understands the most incomprehensible facts and even the thoughts in men's hearts. The Igbo say: *Onwere ihe gbara Chukwu ghari?* 'Is there anything which could come as a surprise to God?' When a person suffers an injustice or is falsely accused, he may in despair exclaim, *Chukwu omuzikwori anya?* 'Is God no longer awake? Why should he let this happen to me?' But he may draw some consolation by repeating, *Chukwu ga ekpe*, 'God will judge'. He sees everything, he will eventually give justice where it is due. This is borne out by many of the names Igbo give to their children:

Chukwuma God knows (what is in the heart)

Chukwumobi God knows what is in the heart or **Chukwumoge** – God knows the time (when my desires will come true)

Chukwufuzulu God sees everything. Nothing is hidden from him

Thus in a sense, the Igbo have some concept of God's ubiquity. This is conceived however, not as all-pervading, but as an effective presence wherever and whenever his help is needed.

The moral attributes of God

Many of the Igbo proverbs and sayings already referred to show that the Igbo do not conceive of God as a remote, impersonal power as some writers have said of the Supreme Being in African traditional religion. He is, rather, a personal being, a conscious being, who knows everything and can reason and decide – who guides and directs the universe according to His inscrutable purpose. By His divine providence, He directs the destiny of every person, even down to the least creature in the world.

More than this however, the Igbo believe that goodness is one of God's essential attributes. Only things which are good, pure, and noble can be – and are – attributed to God. Similarly, nothing which is considered bad, impure, or ignoble can be associated with Him. It is absurd, a contradiction, to predicate any evil of God. One cannot ever say that God is wicked, or that God is unjust, that God is deceptive, or that God is a liar. When the Igbo are in the grips of a crisis, they indeed wonder why God has permitted it, but they say resignedly, *Ọbụ uche Chukwu, ana agbagha ya agbagha*, 'It is God's will, is it ever questioned?' Sympathizers say to the bereaved: *Dibe oh! Oseburuwa emela uche ya* 'Be comforted! God has done His will'. Death is the greatest evil in Igbo experience; but *ọnwụ Chi* – God's death (or natural death) – is never questioned, and sometimes is even seen as an occasion of great rejoicing.[4]

God's moral attributes – His goodness, kindness, mercy, love, justice, and so forth, are acclaimed in many Igbo proverbs, expressions and personal names.

God's Love, Kindness and Mercy

Words and expressions which express gratitude for His

love and kindness are in frequent use in everyday life.
Those who have recently given birth are complimented
with expressions such as these:

Chukwu aluka 'God has worked wonders. God has been
very kind.'

Arinze Chukwu 'Thanks be to God!'
But for God, this child would not have been born to you.

Ekene dili Chukwu 'Thanks be to God!'

Chukwu abuka 'God is so good and kind' (literally 'so great').

Children who are believed to be a special gift from God,
especially when all hope of getting children seem to have
faded, are given names such as these which express God's
mercy and kindness:

Nwa chukwunyere A son given by God
As if to say, only by the mercy of God, could this child have
come to me.

Chukwuemeka God has done well
God has been very kind to me, *Chukwu emekalum*.

Chukwudiogo God is generous.
Liberality in giving without expecting recompense is one of
the virtues most esteemed by the Igbo. *Ime ogo* means simply
to give completely gratis.

Olisaeloka Providence has been very, very kind
This name typically expresses one's intimate experience of
God's mercy and kindness in a wholly unexpected fortune
which comes exactly when one most needs it.

The Justice of God

The Igbo believe that God will judge every good and evil
deed. One who is wronged and cannot obtain redress often
repeats the phrase, *Chukwu ga ekpe* 'God will judge'; or *ka ina
arafu mmadu iga arafu Chukwu*, 'If you succeed in deceiving
men, you cannot deceive God'. A person who has been
falsely accused may say – or name his child – *Chigolum*- 'May
God plead my case'. Such a person may console himself with
Chukwumanjo 'Only God knows what is really evil'.

Recently, after many years of childless marriage, a man –
in despair – got a child outside marriage. He paid the
customary dowry, claimed the child and gave him the name

Chukwu-ma-njǫ 'God knows what is sin'. His wife left him in anger and she too got a child and named him *Chigǫlụm* 'May God plead my case'. A famous Igbo proverb says: *Chukwu bie ikpe, okwu agwụ* 'When God settles an issue it is final'. This proverb is now seen written in English on some lorries, as 'God's case, no appeal'.

Summary and conclusions

The detailed analysis of myths, folk-tales, names, proverbs and sayings in the previous pages have given us much information about the nature and attributes of God. Now, we shall put all this information together and try and draw certain conclusions to represent a synopsis of the Igbo beliefs about God. This will be the nearest we can get to evolving an Igbo theodicy. Devoid of a written language and trained theologians, Igbo traditional religion has not developed a systematic theodicy. God is rather conceived in terms of his activities and his relationship with the universe, the world of the living and the underworld.

The following conclusions may be drawn:

God existed from the beginning. By the 'beginning', the Igbo understand the time when nothing besides God was in existence. They do not talk of – nor could they conceive of – a time when God did not exist. He is eternal. The Igbo mind however, does not stop to speculate how or when God came into existence. There is no concept of God as an *Ens a se*, 'a being existing of itself'. But the Igbo belief that God pre-existed everything warrants the conclusion that He is not dependent on other beings for His existence. Therefore, as an uncaused cause, God is distinct from the world. The Igbo are not pantheists. Igbo mythology, moreover, implies that God created the world from nothing. He is thus the First Cause.

God is omnipotent and transcendent. He is above the world and the deities and above men and the natural forces.

The creative activity of God did not end with creation. He is still very involved with the preservation of the world. God is the Great Providence – Chukwu.

God is also immanent. He is immanent through his Chi in

each person. Human life, destiny, fortunes and misfortunes, and even death are under the control of Chukwu
through his creative emanation, Chi. Every human soul is
immediately created by God at conception.

The Chi which Chukwu gives each person at the moment
of his birth directs him all through life and goes back to
Chukwu at death. Although there is a whole troop of deities
and forces which can terminate man's life prematurely,
death after ripe old age is the end of man's life as ordained
by God. It is therefore *ọnwụ Chi*, God's death.

The charge by J. H. Driberg that what has been called a
Supreme Being in the beliefs of African peoples is in fact
'the concept of a universal power of energy which informs
and is the cause of all life'[5] is not applicable to Chukwu.
From what we have said, it must be abundantly clear that
the Igbo God is a living God, a person. His attributes
include those which presuppose an intelligence and will. He
is loving and kind. He sometimes decides, and at other
times He is believed to judge wrongdoers and mete out
punishments. His favours can sometimes be solicited with
prayers and sacrifices. He is a moral God: on the one hand,
nothing evil can be associated with him – He is upright, just,
and faithful; on the other, He requires good conduct on the
part of his worshippers.

This embryonic Igbo theodicy provides themes for many
Igbo proverbs: *Ngu Chukwu gbunyere onye ka oji ekota ihe*,
'God gives each person a hook to pluck things with'. A man
might pray over kola nut,[6] *Chukwu nyere akụ-oyibo mmili ọna
ara, nye anyi ndụ, nye anyi ihe anyi ga eji akwado ya*, 'May God
who gives the coconut the milk it drinks, give us life and the
wherewithal to support it'. Another proverb expresses
man's total dependence on God, *Chukwu ji ji; jide mma, onye
ọwanyere orie*, 'God has the yam and the knife; only those for
whom he cuts a piece can eat'.

This basic Igbo theodicy is confirmed by the observations
of many writers on Igbo religion. According to Basden,
'circumscribed belief in the Supreme Being and a Future
Life is universal among the Igbo people. They maintain
that He is all powerful and overlords all inferior spirits. His
attributes include beneficence, and He grants favours to
mankind in a general way. As a just God, too, He metes out

punishments for wrong-doing'.[7] Arinze summarizes Igbo theodicy thus: 'God is the Supreme Spirit, the creator of everything. No one equals Him in power. He knows everything. He is altogether a good and merciful God and does harm to no one. He sends rain and especially children, and it is from him that each individual derives his personal Chi. But this Supreme Spirit has made many inferior spirits who are nearer to man and through whom man normally offers worship to Him'.[8]

Notes

1 The term 'theophoric name' means a name composed with an attribute of God.
2 The name of the eleventh king of Nnewi, who reigned over a century before the first missionaries came to Nnewi in 1905, was *Eze-Chukwu* (God is King): cf. Alutu, J. O. *A groundwork of Nnewi History* (1963) p.228. The king Aboh at the time of the second Niger Expedition in 1857 was called *Chukwuma* (God knows everything).
3 Anozia, I. P. 'The Religious Import of Igbo Names', unpublished thesis, Urban University, Rome (1968) p.105.
4 Like many African people, the Igbo have an ancestor cult. There is great rejoicing expressed in elaborate funeral rites when a person dies in good old age of *ọnwụ chi*, God's death.
5 Driberg, J. H. 'The secular aspects of Ancestor Worship in Africa', supplement to *Journal of the Royal African Society*, vol. 35, no. 138 (Jan. 1936). Quoted by Smith, E. W. *African Ideas of God* (1961) p.21.
6 Kola-nuts are nuts produced by the Kola tree common throughout West Africa. They are slightly smaller than pingpong balls, and either crimson or white in colour. Their degree of bitterness varies from species to species. Addicts chew them as excitants, and in company they are passed around from one person to another. Among the Igbo they have important social and ritual significance as we hope to show.
7 Basden, G. T. *Niger Ibos* (1966) p.36.
8 Arinze, F. A. *Sacrifice in Ibo Religion* (1970) p.9.

4 God in the African world-view

From the cosmogonic myths and folk-tales analysed in the foregoing chapters, it is clear that Chukwu holds a central position in Igbo beliefs. He is creator and organizer of the world and its creatures, including the deities. But the cosmogonic stories alone do not give us a clear picture of the world as the Africans see it. Is their world limited to the visible, or is there a realm beyond the visible world? What, according to them, is the structure of the universe? What kinds of beings exist in the world? Have the deities a separate world of their own? What are the relations between the different beings in the world: between God and the world, God and the deities, God and men, the deities and men, the living and the dead? A reply to these questions in some detail would give us insight into the African world-view.

A people's world-view may be defined as the complex of their beliefs and attitudes concerning the origin, nature, structure of the universe and the interaction of its beings — with particular reference to man. It is against this background that the major problems of man are conceived, assessed, and their solutions sought. These include not only the problems connected with his life, his happiness, his fears, the end and purpose of his life, his death and after-life, but also his social and religious institutions.

Writers who try to describe the African world-view often find themselves in a dilemma. If they were to describe the African world-view as it was before contact with Christianity and European cultures, they may find that they are trying to paint a picture which does not represent the beliefs and practices of the people today, and is therefore irrelevant. If, however, they were to describe the African world-view as it is today, this would encompass not only the

traditional beliefs, but other beliefs which have been inte-
grated into the African system, but which can be shown to
be of foreign origin.

Here, the point must be made that although a people's
traditional world-view draws heavily on their surroundings
and their cultural past in the same way that their other
traditional concepts do, it is by no means static. It is constantly being reinterpreted and reformulated in the light of
new experience within the community, and stimuli from
external contacts.

The traditional Igbo world-view is described here as it is
today. Among both Igbo Christians and adherents of the
traditional religion, the traditional world-view is juxtap-
osed with the Christian world-view, so that the ordinary
Igbo belongs to two worlds. He draws from the one or the
other according to circumstances, and easily combines
them. The traditional world-view has changed in some of its
aspects where such influences have been accepted and inte-
grated with the traditional beliefs.

I shall endeavour to discuss some of the basic ideas which
run through the Igbo world-view and give it coherence,
meaning and credibility. These ideas could be said to be the
philosophy of the African world-view. Any world-view
described without its underlying philosophy is presented as
a folk-tale, a mythological story, and to do so is to hold it up
to ridicule. A people's world-view is a significant part of
their system of religious beliefs. Writers who want to do
justice to it should present it as such. They should tell us not
only what the people believe and why they do so, but how all
these beliefs fit together in the logic of those who believe.
Many writers fail to do so and present African beliefs
merely as a medley of superstitions.

Mbari houses – a microcosm of the Igbo world-view

Mbari houses are religious art monuments built in honour
of certain deities in some parts of Igboland. They are usually an expression of thanksgiving by the community to a
deity for great favours received – an abundant harvest, a
high fertility rate: or deliverance from an epidemic. Many

Mbari are built in honour of *Ala*, the Earth Mother, who is regarded as a giver of life, a protector and supreme judge. Sometimes Mbari houses are built for other deities, especially *Amadiọha*, a sky deity associated with thunder, to celebrate spectacular successes like victory in war.

It is up to the priest to know when his deity desires or demands an Mbari. He ascertains this through divination or other traditionally accepted ways. He then selects some young men and women who are said to be specially invited by the deity, to build him an Mbari. These go into seclusion in an enclosure around the shrine of the deity or any other place he has selected for his Mbari. The seclusion may last from nine months to two years, depending on how long it takes to complete the work.[1]

When completed, an Mbari is a microcosm of the Igbo world-views; in it is found a selection of the different beings and events characteristic of this Igbo world-view. In the centre of the Mbari house is usually a giant-size mud statue of *Ala*, the Earth-mother, majestically seated on her mud throne with her two children, one on either side. Other deities sit on the other sides of the house or on their Mbari; there are *Amadiọha*, the deity of thunder, *Ekwunoche*, a river spirit – giver of children; *Njoku*, deity of yams; *Agwụnsi*, divination deity, and numerous local spirits. Creatures from mythology, nature and the underworld also people Mbari houses. *Mamy Wata*, an imported water spirit, is shown squatting in a corner with her snake pots, a cross around her neck. Strangers to the Igbo world are well represented. The white man who long ago mysteriously appeared from nowhere is sometimes shown coming up from a hole in the ground.[2] His new rôle as the colonial master is symbolically represented by a General looking down through an upstairs window. Thus, side by side with the mystical world, the Mbari endeavour to represent every human experience old and new.

The Mbari houses illustrate four main characteristics of the traditional African and Igbo world-view: the multiplicity of spiritual beings; the unity of their world-view – there is no dichotomy between the spiritual and the material world; the hierarchical order of beings; and the essential connection and interaction between beings.

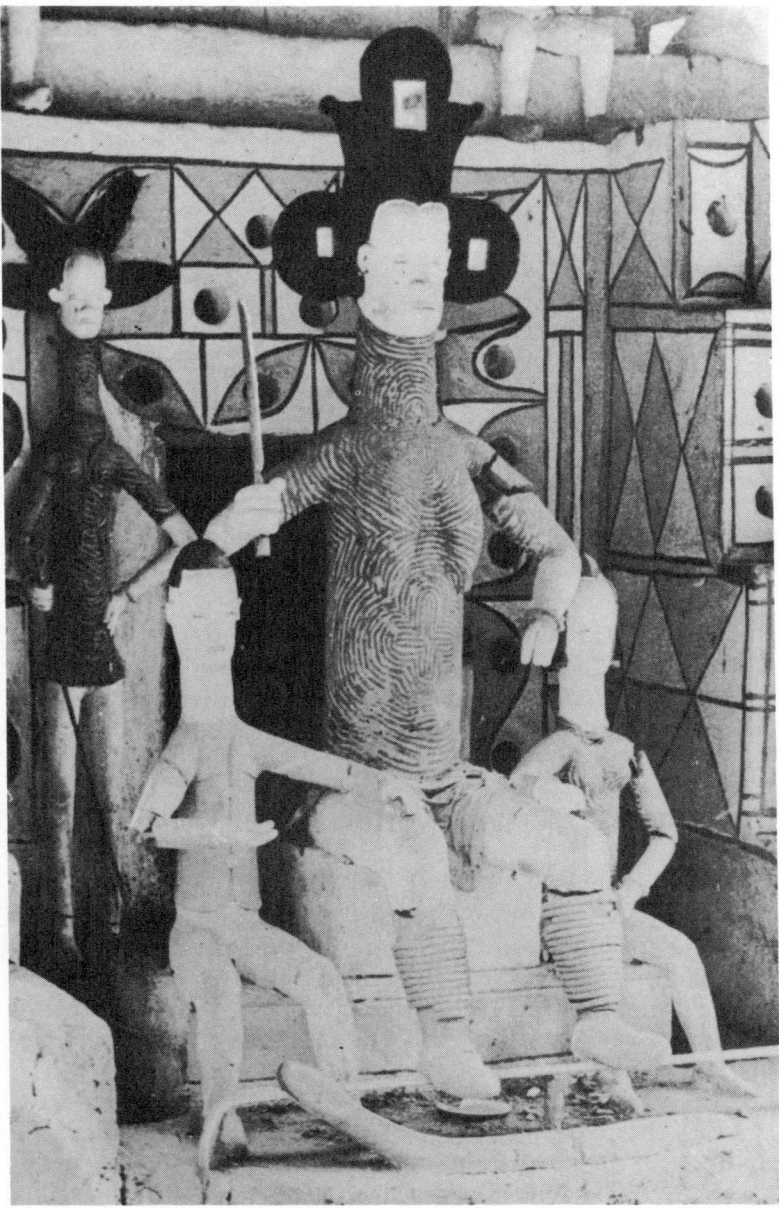

Plate 3 An imposing image of Ala (Earth Mother) sitting at the centre of an Mbari house

The multiplicity of spiritual beings

Generally, there are a vast number of spiritual beings in the traditional African world-view. Perhaps this is more true of West Africans than of the Bantu-speaking peoples of East and Central Africa, for many writers have noted a significant difference between the two world-views. 'In their cosmology,' writes Edwin Smith, 'the Bantu appear to give a lesser place than the Sudanese Negroes to these nature spirits. The spirits of the Bantu are mostly those of human beings who continue to live in the unseen world.'[3] The few nature spirits are for the most part personifications of natural phenomena. In West Africa where nature is full of vitality, these natural spirits are numbered in their hundreds. The enormous number of Yoruba deities is symbolically presented by an Ifa divination verse which speaks of 'The one thousand four-hundred-and-four divinities'.[4]

The world – as the Igbo know it – is full of spirits. Their world is not limited to the material world of visible beings but includes the realm of invisible things. Nobody who has been to the country of the Igbo entertains any doubts about this. 'Every Igbo,' writes Fr. Jordan, 'believed that an invisible universe was in action all around him, and that his term of life was short if he happened to fall foul of its denizens'.[5]

The unity of the Igbo world-view

However, the vast number of spiritual beings does not imply that the dichotomy found in European philosophy and theology between the material and the spiritual, the visible and the invisible, the sacred and the profane, exists in Igbo traditional religion. Here, as in many other instances, the use of western terminology far from adequately expressing African concepts, distorts them. Mbari houses bear out the essential unity of the Igbo world-view.

The Igbo world is one, not two. The invisible beings, the deities and the spirits have no separate world of their own, different from that of human experience. God as we saw, is imagined to live in *Ezi Chukwu*, God's compound, far distant in the outer space, but it is still contained in this world or universe. The ancestors inhabit *Ani mmụọ*, land of the spirits, which is believed to be inside the ground where the ancestors lie buried. Igbo divinities are very much linked with nature and natural phenomena. Deities are believed to inhabit certain physical phenomena with which they are associated. Anyanwụ, the sun, a deity, inhabits the sun, which is also called *Anyanwụ*. Igwe, the sky deity, inhabits the sky, *Igwe*. Amadiọha, linked with thunder and lightning, is also a sky deity. Sometimes the Igbo see the sun or the sky as physical expressions of Chukwu, so that if one were to reproduce the topography of the 'invisible world' by considering the abodes of the deities, it would be a carbon copy of the visible world.

Just as there is the all-pervading sky above, and the extensive ground below, so there is Chukwu, the Supreme Being, in the heavens, and Ala, the Earth-mother, below. Great and powerful deities such as Anyanwụ, Igwe and Amadiọha serve Chukwu above, just as large heavenly bodies decorate the sky, while Ala, the Earth-mother, presides as queen over the innumerable deities inhabiting the rivers, the mountains, the caves, the forest, and the many other spirit forces found on the earth. The Ancestors, *Ndichie*, inhabit *Ala mmụọ*, the spirit-land, which is located somewhere in the ground, so they come under Ala. Similarly man, *mmadụ*, is not a composite being of body *and* soul. The body is only the visible expression of the real person – *onye ahụ*. What subsists after death is not a part of man or the soul, but the person. Unlike the soul, the person after death is imagined to be of the same stature, age and status as the living person. In the same way, God has not created two worlds one visible and the other invisible; rather, both visible and invisible beings co-exist and interact in the one world which God has created. The evaluation of beings is not based on whether they are visible or invisible, material or spiritual. The spiritual beings are not necessarily all good, or the most powerful. When man dies he goes to the spirit-land *Ala mmụọ*, but reaching it is not man's final end. Man's world goes in a cycle as we shall see. An ancestor in the spirit-land wants to be reincarnated and reappear again and again, thus enjoying both the visible and invisible worlds.

The hierarchy of beings

Beings, in the Igbo world-view, are not all of the same kind, nor are they of equal importance. They are differentiated according to their kind and importance. They can accordingly be arranged in a hierarchy, depending on their power and the rôle they play in the ontological order in nature. All beings known in the Igbo hierarchy can be grouped into five categories: *Okike*, Creator, *Mmụọ*, deities, *Arụsi*, spirit-forces, *Ndi Mmụọ*, disembodied human spirits and *Ụwa*, the material, physical world.

1   Chukwu, *Creator*

First in the hierarchy, Chukwu, the Creator (*Okike*) of everything, transcends the world, and at the same time is immanent through the deities, who are His messengers and representatives in nature; and especially through *Chi* – the spirit-guardians regarded as manifestations of Himself which reside in every creature.

2   Mmụọ, *deities*

Next come the deities. The Igbo term *Mmụọ* is not adequate because it also literally covers all invisible beings including the Creator, the Arụsi, and the Ancestors, but since all the others have specific names, we shall reserve *Mmụọ* for them. Popular language sometimes refers to the deities as *Arụsi*. But Arụsi belong to a different category of beings, as we shall learn. Nor could the deities justifiably be called 'gods' as is common in popular language and in some other books on African religion. If we do so, it will give the misleading impression that the deities in African religion are conceived in the same way as the gods of Graeco-Roman paganism. Rather, the Igbo deities form the great circle of non-human spirits, who come next to God in the ontological hierarchy and are believed to be his agents, helping Him to shepherd different sections of His creation. Some have their abode in the sky and are believed to be very near Chukwu; others live below and come under Ala, the Earth-mother. However, the deities are more often conceived with reference to the services they render to man; Chukwu who created them, assigned them specific functions. Anyanwu̱, the sun, brings good fortune; Ala herself is the custodian of law and morality and guarantor of political stability. Chi assures fertility and provides guidance and protection; Agwu̱ is the deity of medicine and is also responsible for spirit possession, prophecy and divination. O̱fo̱ is a symbol of justice, Ikenga symbolizes the strength of a man's right hand and brings him good luck and success. Ekwensu, often identified with the devil, provokes people to violence and is therefore invoked during wars.

3 Aru̱si, *spirit-forces*

Although we used the term 'spirits' to translate *Aru̱si*, they are not fully personal and may be better described as spirit-forces. They sometimes act irrationally and this distinguishes them from the deities. An informant, Nweke Ezeamalu of Oba, explained the difference between the deities and Aru̱si thus: 'whenever you invoke Aru̱si on somebody, it blindly kills him whether he is at fault or not'. The Aru̱si are numbered in hundreds. Besides its deities, each village has its pantheon of Aru̱si. An Aru̱si can be the property of a clan, a family, or even an individual. An informant explained to me that an Aru̱si can be man-made, but usually an object becomes an Aru̱si when a spirit begins to manifest itself through it. Divination confirms that such an object has become the permanent abode of a spirit-force.

4 Ndi Mmu̱o̱, *disembodied spirits*

This is the army of disembodied spirits of the dead. The spirits of good men who have reached *Ala Mmu̱o̱*, the spirit-land are *Ndichie*, Ancestors. The spirits of evil men, and all who have not reached *Ani Mmu̱o̱*, roam around restlessly in *Ama Nri Mmu̱o̱ na Mmadu̱*, an intermediate state between the spirit-land and the visible world of men. These are evil spirits, and include *Akalogeli, Qgbǫnuke, Qgbanje* etc. Associated with evil spirits are *Amusu*, witches, and *Qgwu*, medicine men.

5 Ụwa, *the visible world*

The visible world is the world of daily experience. It consists of the sky above and the earth below. It is the world of man and of human institutions. Man lives out most of his cycle of life in the visible world. His birth, his life in society, his death, his reincarnation, all take place in this life. Only a tiny fraction of this life-cycle, i.e. his brief and temporary sojourn in the ancestral world, takes place in the invisible world. This may be one of the reasons why African traditional religion is life-affirming rather than life-denying. Long life with prosperity, plenty of children, wives, and a large number of relatives and friends, is a sign of blessedness, and consequently the constant theme of prayers and petitions to God and the deities. This theme, which is very central to African traditional religion, will be developed further later in this book.

The interaction of beings

It would be wrong to think that invisible beings interact only among themselves. There is a continuous exchange between all the beings in the Igbo world-view, irrespective of the class of being (visible or invisible) to which they belong. Men can be possessed by spirits and spirits sometimes incarnate themselves in visible form. Men can influence the deities and the spirits through sacrifices, prayers and spells. Conversely, the deities can intervene in human affairs to bring order and blessings, or they can upset the human order whenever their laws are not obeyed. All the beings in the Igbo world-view are linked together by a network or relationships guided by fixed laws, *ǫmenala*. Any deviation from these laws by one being, even inadvertently, can upset the order and bring disaster for others. This explains the frequent incidence of sacrifices in Igbo religion and the

numerous and apparently trivial offences for which cleansing sacrifices are required. Offences which disrupt the
natural order are called *Arụ*, literally, abominations. But in
Igbo usage the word has the connotation – 'crime against
nature'. Such offences require the elaborate cleansing
ceremony of *Ikpụ Arụ* – removing any abomination and
restoring the natural order. A list of these offences shows
that they can be perpetrated unconsciously or involuntar-
ily.

A man having sexual intercourse with his father's wife
Abortion
A man committing suicide
Sexual intercourse with an animal
The birth of twins
A child cutting its upper teeth before the lower
A hen hatching but one chick.[6]

All these are *Arụ*, because the Igbo believe that they transgress the laws guiding the ontological order and will therefore bring disaster to the community. The emphasis is not
on guilt but on the disturbance of the natural order. The
Igbo say, *Ahụbe bụ Arụ*, 'Abnormality is an abomination'.
The birth of twins is abnormal because men are usually
born one at a time. Twins are therefore a threat to the
natural order and must be destroyed.

   According to Tempels, this outlook is based on the African notion of being. Africans conceive beings as living
forces. *Being* is always *active*, dynamic not static. Beings are
linked with one another by a network of relationships like a
spider's web and the action of one affects the whole. Since
being is a living force, interaction between beings may lead
either to the reinforcement of the power of being, or its
diminution. These are some of the assumptions of Bantu
philosophy as enunciated by Tempels. 'In the minds of
Bantu,' writes Tempels, 'all beings in the universe possess
vital force of their own: human, animal, vegetable or
inanimate. Each being has been endowed by God with a
certain force capable of strengthening the vital energy of
the strongest being of all creation: man'.[7] One may indeed
question some of the details inherent in this theory, or
Tempels' formulation of them. For example, one may ques-

tion his contention that 'Force is even more than a necessary attribute of beings. Force is the nature of being, force is being, being is force.'[8] It is difficult even by a great mental effort, to see how *force* could be identical with *being*, and not an attribute, albeit an essential one.

Nevertheless, the concept of *being* as interacting living forces is fundamental to the traditional African world-view. This is true not only of Bantu-speaking Africa but also of some other areas, as is illustrated by the rite of *ituju Ala*. This Igbo rite of 'cooling the land' is performed before erecting any new building. It involves offerings and libations to cool the land force and to win the favour of other beings having a vital relationship to the land. This rule assures one who has come to make his home on a piece of land that he is in the right relationship with the land force, with other beings (e.g. the ancestors), and with forces which are in dynamic relationship with that piece of land. As with the Ashanti, so with the Igbo; before certain trees are cut down they may be propitiated with offerings and addressed as follows, 'I am about to cut you down and carve you; do not let me suffer harm'.[9] Offerings are often made on wooden drums, farm implements, weapons of war or yam seedlings to cool the life force in them and make them more effective in the service they render to their users. These examples seem to bear out the belief in a spider's web of vital relationships between beings: what happens to any part affects the whole. This is part of the ontological order established by God.

We have dwelt at length on this aspect of the traditional African world-view because it explains the dynamics of traditional religion. It provides a key to the understanding of their worship, worship responses, morality and even their ideas about the afterlife. The relationship of God to the different beings in the traditional world-view will be discussed in the following two chapters.

Notes

1 Talbot, P. A. *Some Nigerian Fertility Cults* (1967) p.10.

2 *African Arts*, African Studies Center, University of California.
3 Smith, E. W. *African Ideas of God* (1961) p.3.
4 Idowu, B. *Olodumare, God in Yoruba Belief* (1962) p.3.
5 Jordan, J. P. *Bishop Shanahan of Southern Nigeria* (1971) p.117.
6 Basden, G. T. *Niger Igbos* (1966) p.262.
7 Tempels, P. *Bantu Philosophy* (1969) p.58.
8 Tempels, P. ibid. (1969) p.46.
9 Busia, K. A. 'The Ashanti', in Forde, Daryll (ed.) *African Worlds* (1968), pp.194ff.

5 God, the deities and spirit forces

Spiritual beings in the Igbo world-view can be broadly divided into two categories – non-human and human. Non-human spirits form the first three categories of the Igbo ontological hierarchy. First is *Chukwu*, Creator; next come the deities, *Mmụọ,* and then the spirit-forces, *Arụsi*. This chapter examines the relationship between beings in these three categories.

The Igbo recognize some relationship between Chukwu and Mmụọ, the deities but their conception of this relationship is not very clear. God created the world and infinitely transcends it. He created the deities and is far above them in power and excellence, and yet the deities have divine attributes and receive worship which shows recognition of their divine nature. This is a fact about African traditional religion which anybody with Judeo-Christian background would find most perplexing. If African religion is monotheistic, how do we explain the deities? If it is polytheistic, how can one explain the high monotheistic concepts found in their beliefs? This paradox of the unity and multiplicity of the Divinity is seen in the religious systems of many African societies and may well be a characteristic feature of African traditional religion as a whole.

The Ashanti of Ghana, for example, believe that the world is full of divine beings. The Supreme Being, *Onyankopon*, who created all things, manifests his power through a pantheon of deities, *abosom*. According to Ashanti beliefs, the *abosom* derive their power from the Supreme Being. 'They come from him and are parts of him. A god is but the mouthpiece of the Supreme Being (*Onyankopon Kyeame*) a servant acting as intermediary between Creator and creature.'[1]

Similarly, for the Nuer, *Kwoth Nhial*, the Supreme Spirit, is the creator and mover of all things. Under God there are lesser spirits which can be classified into two groups: *Kuth nhial*, spirits of the sky or of above; and *Kuth piny*, spirits of the earth who are the most powerful of all the lesser spirits and thought to be the children of God. The form the Nuer use to express this relationship, *gaat Kwoth*, sons or children of God, is a clear indication that these spirits are regarded as something lesser and lower than Father-God. They are not regarded as creative spirits as is God but as beings that derive from him. Thus they are both distinct from and identical with God. 'They are many but also one; God is manifested and in a sense *is*, each of them.' Evans-Pritchard expressed his perception of the paradox thus: 'I receive the impression that in sacrificing or in singing hymns to an air spirit, Nuer do not think that they are communicating with the spirit and not with God. They are, if I have understood the matter correctly, addressing God in a particular spiritual figure or manifestation.'[2]

The Yoruba Supreme Being, *Olodumare*, is the Creator, Lord and Father of the deities, *Orisha*. At the beginning *Olodumare* lived with the *Orisha* in the heavens. He it was who sent them down to earth with different assignments to perform, giving them responsibility for supervising different parts of the universe and different aspects of human life. The *Orisha* are therefore regarded as his deputies and messengers.[3]

For the Igbo, similarly, this paradox presents no problem. They see no contradiction in accepting one Creator of all things and at the same time recognizing many deities. Chukwu is not a jealous God. On the contrary, it would seem that in line with their ideas about kingship and nobility, the number and power of the subordinate deities enhance the importance and supremacy of Chukwu, just as the prestige of a king is sometimes measured by the number and power of his subordinate chiefs. So it would be normal and logical to the Igbo to affirm in one breath the unity and supremacy of God, and the greatness and multiplicity of the deities. This is very well illustrated by the Igbo morning prayer, *Igo Oji Ututu,* during which God, the deities, the spirits, and the ancestors are invoked according to their order and rank, and are invited to participate in the kola communion:

Chineke taa Oji	God eat kola
Chukwu Abiama ta Oji	God of the universe eat kola
Anyanwu na Ezenu taa Oji	Sun, and King of the sky eat kola
Ala ekene!	Earth deity greeting!
Igwe ekene!	Sky deity greeting!
Taa nu Oji	Eat kola
Nde mbu, Nde abuo,	First, second, ancestors
Nde ekere ato	Up to last three generations
Nna Nnaa ha	Great grandfathers
Taa nu Oji	Eat kola (and so on).[4]

But what exactly is the rôle of deities in relation to the Supreme Being? Igbo beliefs are very clear about it. Chukwu is distinct from the world and believed to be as distant from it as the sky is distant from the earth. All creatures, including the deities, are *in* the world and that is where their activities take place. They are thought to reside in different natural phenomena. They are there as God's representatives or, as the Igbo say, His sons or messengers, just as God Himself is present in every person through his Chi. As spirits, the deities are believed to have easier access to God, yet heaven is not viewed as a court where the deities and the ancestors act as councillors and courtiers. Rather, the deities are like administrators in distant provinces. They administer different sectors of creation and report regularly to Chukwu. God is thus transcendent but at the same time immanent in creation through the spirits.

The deities enjoy a great measure of sovereignty and independence in the aspect of life over which they have charge. Sometimes they are offered acts of worship and in prayers are credited with attributes which those with Christian or Moslem monotheistic traditions would think belonged to God alone. However, Igbo beliefs generally emphasize that ultimate power and authority rest with God. This ambivalent aspect of the relationship between God and deities is very well illustrated by the information given to me by Okafor Awali. He told me that my grandfather, Ezeana Nnewi, was very devoted to an *Arusi* called

Ogwugwu. When people get sick, especially young important members of the community, he would bring the image
of the Arụsi, and after the rites of breaking kola, he would
pray aloud, his voice arising in crescendo:

Ogwugwu emecha nka ọfọ one	Ogwugwu, if this dies how many will be left?
Ogwugwu ekwena	Ogwugwu please don't let it happen!
Ogwugwu emecha nka one afọ	Ogwugwu, if this goes how many will be left?[5]

And Okafor concluded, if God did not want him after this,
Ogwugwu would save him. This story demonstrates how
the power of Ogwugwu over the life and death of the sick
person is conditioned by the power and authority of God.

We shall now discuss the relationship between Chukwu
and a select number of the most important deities. All the
deities are not related to Chukwu in the same way, and each
different relationship between God and the deity is expressed differently both in language and in ritual.

Anyanwụ (sun)

The cult of Anyanwụ is widespread in Igboland. In some
areas, Anyanwụ is confused with or even identified with
Chukwu, the Supreme Being.[6] Such phrases as *Anyanwụ Eze
Chukwu Okike*, The Sun, the Lord, God the Creator, seem to
refer to a single personality.[7] Some title-names for God in
different areas include the name for Anyanwụ, Sun. In the
Awka area for example, a favourite name for God is *Anyanwụ na Agbala*, The Sun, and the Great Deity, while the
name *Anyanwụ na Ezenu*, The Sun and King of the Heavens,
is very commonly used. These two names seem to imply a
composite personality, but I am told that they refer to a
single being – the Supreme Being. If pressed, however,
they will readily admit that Anyanwụ is the son or messenger of God. When I put this question to Ezeana, the
chief priest of Umudioka village in Awka, he answered, 'It is
the same God who made man who is also called *Anyanwụ na
Agbala*; *Ọbụ ife eji emeju okwu* – it is a supplementary appel-

lation. Chukwu is the creator and maker of the world, *Anyanwu na Agbala* are like his messengers.' When I pressed on and suggested that they are not therefore one, he replied, 'Don't you see that having begotten a son who does messages for him, both have become one?'[8] This may not sound logical, but the Christian doctrine of the hypostatic union is no more logical. It is a matter of belief not of reason. Anyanwu, therefore, is called the 'son of Chineke', and sometimes is referred to as His emanation.

Anyanwu is regarded in a special way as a deity bringing wealth and good fortune. His altar consists of an *Ora* or *Ogilisi* (*Newbouldia*) tree, at the foot of which a small mound of red clay is fashioned, into which a round pottery dish is sunk bottom downwards. This dish which usually contains some sacrificial water is called *oku awele*, vessel of fortune. Before a man goes to market, he may pour a little palm wine into the bowl of Anyanwu, dip his fingers in the bowl, touch his tongue with his fingers, and say, 'I am going to market; may Anyanwu grant that my words may sound sweet to those with whom I trade'.[9] A diviner would recommend a sacrifice to Anyanwu to someone who is in the habit of dissipating his wealth.

Igwe, Amadioha or Kamalu (sky deities)

Just as a husband fertilizes his wife, so Igwe, in the form of rain, fertilizes Ala, the Earth Deity. Yet, the cult of Igwe is popular only in certain parts of Igboland, particularly in the south. In such places, his power is celebrated in praise-names such as *Igwe-ka-Ala*, 'heaven greater than the earth'. Igwe is regarded as the agent of Chineke against unde-tected criminals. He expresses his power and anger in thunderbolts and lightning.[10]

In many places, thunder and lightning themselves are worshipped as deities under the names *Amadioha* or *Kamalu*. Those struck down by lightning are not mourned because God is believed to have punished them for their sins through his just agent, Amadioha. In very serious disputes involving false and malicious accusations, Chukwu is sometimes called upon to arbitrate through Amadioha.[11]

Plate 4 Amadiọha (Deity of Thunder) with his wife sitting on their Mbari

This involves a simple ritual. A white cock is taken to Amadiọha's shrine tied to a bamboo stick which is then stuck in the ground before the shrine. The offender is asked to declare his innocence and then break an egg before the shrine of Amadiọha. This part of the ritual is called *itu ogu*. If he is innocent, it is believed that thunder and lightning will fight for his cause. The head of the cock is torn off the body and placed at the shrine. The Supreme God is expected to act unfailingly through his agent, Amadiọha.[12]

Long before the colonization of Igboland, a shrine of Igwe at Umunnọha in the Owerri division, and another of Kamalu at Ozuzu developed into very powerful oracles whose fame spread far beyond the confines of Igboland. The owners of the cult in time took it upon themselves to impose death penalties 'under the guidance of Igwe' on supposed criminals.[13] The colonial government suppressed them.

Ala, Ana (Earth Deity)[14]

Just as Chukwu presides over the sky deities, so Ala (Earth Deity) is believed to preside over the deities below. Ala is regarded as the owner of men, alive or dead. The cult of the Ancestors is therefore closely associated with that of the Earth Deity, who is queen of the underworld.[15] In fact, the Igbo sometimes speak as if God and Ala equally share responsibility for the universe. Sometimes, when somebody is seriously sick, it is said of him, '*ọnọ ikpe be Chukwu na Ala*', he is on trial before God and the Earth Deity. If he recovers, he is said to have won his case against his Ancestors who want to recall him from among the living.

Nevertheless, the cult of Ala is very dear and important to the Igbo. Meek has pointed out that Ala, not Chukwu, Anyanwụ or Amadiọha, is the most important deity in Igbo public and private cults. She is the giver of fertility to men, animals, and crops. Men are born on the earth, they feed on the products of the earth and when they die, they are buried in the earth. Hence, an Igbo funeral song sings:

Ana nwe mmadụ nine   Earth Mother owns men
Ana nwe mmadụ   The Earth owns everybody.[16]

Ala is the source and custodian of *ọmenani* – customs and traditions, and public morality. Accordingly, she exercises the main ritual sanctions in disputes and offences. Crimes such as adultery, incest, homicide, unnatural birth, e.g. birth of twins and so forth are all offences against Ala, the Earth Deity. They are therefore called *Nsọ Ala*, taboos of the Earth Deity. Sanctions for such crimes include propitiatory sacrifices to Ala.

The cult of Ala is one of the most powerful integrating forces in Igbo societies which are characterized by the absence of centralized political authority. Her cult is organized at the family, village and clan level, so that there are family shrines, village shrines and clan shrines to Ala. Public rites are performed at various stages of the farming cycle, and whenever divination indicates. Beautiful paintings and statues abound, representing Ala as giver of fertility, especially in the famous Mbari houses.

Numerous lesser spirits like Ifejioku, Agwụ, and the innumerable *Arụsi*, or local spirits of rivers, forests, personifications of fortune, wealth, luck, and so forth are conceived as subordinate to Ala.

Ifejioku

Ifejioku is the deity protector of the yam, the main food of the Igbo. Even though Ifejioku is subordinate to Ala, the Earth Deity and collaborates with her, it is not an *Arusi*. The cult of Ifejioku is widespread throughout Igboland. In some places it is called *Njoku* or *Ajoku*. Sacrifices are made to Ifejioku before the planting season, and soon after the harvesting of new yams.

Agwụ

Agwụ is the patron spirit of divination and diviners. It is called *mmụọ nkpasa*, spirit of confusion. Agwụ chooses its worshippers and endows them with the gift of divination and the knowledge of medicinal herbs. Agwụ afflicts its victims with psychological disturbance which sometimes takes the form of restlessness, wastefulness or even madness – *Ara Agwụ*. Hence if you ask somebody *Agwụ ọna akpa gi?*, 'Are you seized by Agwụ?' it is just like saying, 'Are you mad?' The rite of *ilụ Agwụ* or *Ikpu Agwụ*, tying up or covering up Agwụ, should not only bring the victim back to normality, but should also harness the power of Agwụ in him for the practice of divination and healing with herbs.

Personified attributes of God as deities

There is a set of deities which seem to constitute a group apart. These include Chi, Ikenga, and Ofo. They differ from the other deities in that they are not associated with any natural phenomenon, but rather have such a direct and close link with God that they appear to be personifications of one or other of His divine attributes. Thus the deity Chi is the personification of the divine providence as it exists in and directs each individual; Ikenga symbolizes God's assistance in the realization of manly achievements, while Ofo is a symbol of divine justice and authority.

Chi

The controversial deity Chi, and its close associate Eke, as the Igbo conceive them are certainly personifications of different aspects of the divine creative activity. Creation is not a simple and undefinable activity accomplished by a single divine *fiat*. It seems to be rather a multiple act shared by Chukwu, Chi and Eke. God creates the individual, and gives him a Chi and an Eke. The Chi chooses the child's destiny from the many parcels of fortune put before it by Chukwu. Eke lets the child out into the world – *inyo uwa*, giving him at the same time his personality. These points will be further developed in the next chapter, but put simply, Chukwu gives each person existence, his Chi gives him his destiny, and Eke gives him his personality. Hence Horton's apt remark

'When invoking the Supreme Being, the people of Ibagwa frequently allude to the trinity, Chukwu, Ci, and Okuke with the phrase *Eze Citoke*, 'Lord, Ci, Creator'. This trinity emphasizes at once the remote and near aspects of the Ibo concept of God.'[17]

However, the creative rôles of Chi and Eke are secondary and subordinate to that of Chukwu. They are themselves creatures of God, and their creative rôle is limited to choosing the destiny and personality of the individual. In fact, it is believed that once Chi and Eke make their choices, they are irrevocably sealed and indelibly and immutably imprinted by the creator on the palms of the person's hands, the *Akala Aka* or *Akala Chi*, the sign on the palm, or the signs of Chi. A skilled diviner can read a person's fortunes by interpreting the lines on his palms. An Igbo proverb says: *ofu nne na amụ, ma ofu chi adaghi eke*, 'no two persons have the same destiny, not even two brothers'. However, on a very special request from Chi, the Creator may change one or two details of his allotted fortunes. The Igbo say: *Onye kwe chi ya ekwe*, 'if you are persistent, your Chi will go along with you'.

The functions of Chi and Eke do not end with their creative rôles. Chi, like a guardian angel, accompanies and watches over a person all through his life. With paternal care, it judiciously dispenses the contents of the parcel of fortune for the overall welfare of the child. The Igbo believe that Chi is good and goads a person on to good conduct by admonitions, rewards and punishments. Talbot has noted rightly that:

'The Chi always looks after his child and his family and he tries to prevent him from doing bad things.

A man especially prays to Chi when (he is) in trouble or sickness but the latter may get tired of a child who is always doing wrong'.[18]

Such is the solicitude of Chi for its child that the Igbo say: *Nwata mụba iri elu, chi ya achiri uche n'aka*, 'When a child begins to learn how to climb, his Chi becomes very anxious'. Their unshakeable confidence in Chi is expressed by the proverbs: *Mgbo ada egbu onye nya na Chi ya yi*, 'Bullets do not kill a person who is with his Chi', and *Onwụ agagh egbu onye chi ya ga azọ, ọnwụ agagh ahapụ onye Chi ya ga egbu*, 'Death cannot kill a person whom his chi wants to save, nor can death leave a person whom Chi wants to kill'.

There is no doubt that for the Igbo, the transcendent God, who lives in *ezi Chukwu*, God's compound, far away in the sky, becomes immanent through his emanations Chi and Eke which are in men.[19]

Ikenga

Ikenga is a deity whose rôle is very similar to that of Chi. It symbolizes the strength of a man's right hand, so that a man's right hand is sometimes called *Aka Ikenga*, Ikenga hand, or the powerful hand. Ikenga is essentially a human male's deity. Women do not have Ikenga. Rather, they have a great devotion to Chi, guardian deity, who is believed to procure fertility, the greatest aspiration of a woman. Ikenga on the other hand guards a man and inspires in him courage, strength, ambition and achievement – all prerequisites for the success of every man of status.

Accordingly, Ikenga is invoked under the title of *Ikenga ọwa ọta*, that is, 'Ikenga who splits shields', hence the strong one or the brave one. The carved image of the Ikenga represents the deity as a man with two long horns, sitting on a stool, with a drawn sword in his left hand and a human skull in the other. These are emblems of courage and prowess with which the deity is associated.

If a man achieves something manly, for example if he gets a baby boy or builds a house, he attributes this success to his Ikenga. The Ibo expression, *Ikenga kwụ ọtọ tata*, literally 'my Ikenga is standing upright today' is another way of saying that many successes have come his way.

Among the household deities, Ikenga holds the premier rank. No householder can be considered fully settled without it. A household set up without its guardianship and protection would drift aimlessly to an inevitable doom. It is therefore the first deity a person acquires and it retains its foremost place throughout his life. At death, it is split into two, the right half is buried with the owner, and the left half is cast away. This practice shows that the Igbo, like most

Plate 5 Ikenga (Deity of Fortune) holding a heavy club and a human head, symbols of power

Africans, do not worship idols or the carved image of a deity. The idols are not identified with the deities, but are only symbols of them.

There is a very close connection between Ikenga and Chukwu. The Igbo belief is that Ikenga is a guardian deity given by Chukwu to men to help them protect and rear their families. They are very insistent that it is not an Arụsi, or personified natural force. Nweke Ezeamalu was very emphatic that Ikenga is not an Arụsi. *Ọgwụ adirọ ya*, 'there are no charms in it. Why we pray to Ikenga is to give us children'.[20] According to Jeffreys 'The old men at Umuleri declared that so far from Ikenga being an Alụsi – it was synonymous with Tsineke, the Supreme Being'.[21]

The rôle of the spirit-forces (Arụsi)

Besides the deities, *Mmụọ*, there are other spiritual beings which are worshipped by the Igbo. They are called *Ụmụ Arụsi*, spirits.

In the broad context of African traditional religion, Arụsi can be designated as godlings, minor deities, demons, or perhaps more appropriately, spirit-forces. They are numbered in hundreds and find their abode in mysterious rocks, caves, mountains, lakes, rivers, forests and animals. They are endowed with supernatural powers which may sometimes benefit the lucky ones and those initiated into the secrets of their cult. But generally they are ferocious and ruthless and inspire great fear and extreme caution.

Arụsi share some of the attributes of the deities, but differ essentially from them in that they sometimes act irrationally but not immorally. An Arụsi indiscriminately kills anybody who infringes any of its laws, even if he acted inadvertently. Its reaction is automatic. This would be a blasphemous thing to say of God or a deity. It is enough to know the formula and art of controlling Arụsi to bring them into use. Arụsi exist for the good of society. They fight the physical and moral evils in society. Some Arụsi have rituals which ward off misfortunes, fight witchcraft and execute judgement on unidentified criminals. In this sense they have a sort of in-built morality. This can be explained by their origin and nature.

The Igbo conceive Arụsi as 'metaphysical forces' which God created and left in nature. Where favourable conditions exist, they take up their abode in a material object and begin to act through it. In this process of incarnation, they acquire varying degrees of consciousness and power. Fortunate people, especially the *dibia* or diviners who first discover these Arụsi, bond themselves to their service and thus become the owners of the Arụsi. Hence an Arụsi is usually the property of a clan, a village, a family or even an individual. An Arụsi gains recognition as soon as it begins to appear by divination.

Only a few years ago, in 1973, I witnessed a celebration of the discovery of a new Arụsi, *Akpụ*, 'cassava tuber'. We were holding a meeting in a mission station when a crowd of women trooped past the station dancing and singing and waving cassava leaves in the air. The story had it that some cassava tubers had miraculously spoken somewhere on the western side of the Niger, claiming that the widespread disease which had destroyed the cassava crops that year was a punishment because the Arụsi, the spirit of cassava, was never worshipped.[22] After the procession, the women set up a shrine, gathered a heap of cassava before it and invited a priest who made an offering of a fowl, an egg and some palm oil to the new Arụsi, *Akpụ*.

There are hundreds of Arụsi. Each village-group, each clan, has its own pantheon and their number is continually on the increase. Some acquire countrywide fame for a season and soon fall into oblivion. The more ancient ones become the spirit patron of the group which owns them. Like the gods and goddesses of ancient Greece and Rome, the Arụsi are given to scandalous marital unions and immoral practices.

In Nnewi for example, where there are hundreds of Arụsi, they include *Eze Mewi*, the chief Arụsi said to have been brought by the original settlers of Nnewi. There are many emanations of *Ogwugwu*. Most kindreds have their own Ogwugwu to afford protection and bring fertility. Others are Arụsi representing the four days of the Igbo week: Nweke, Nwafor, Nwankwo, Nwoye. Arụsi of rivers include Edo, Idemili, Ulasi, Ụbụ, Ele, Ojiyi. Other Arusi inhabit trees: Akpu (silk cotton), Ojukwu (African cedar),

Ngwu. Others are Aṛọ (year spirit), Udo, Mkpukpa, Usukpe, Ezumezu, Mgbodo, Ufo and so forth.[23]

Although Eze Mewi is still held to be the chief Aṛusi because it was brought in by the original settlers of Nnewi, yet in the ritual, and in the liturgical calendar, it is Edo and not Eze Mewi who gets the most attention. This fact is explained in an Nnewi myth: The chief Aṛusi, Eze Mewi, divorced his first wife, Ogwugwu Ezekwuabo, and married Edo the beautiful daughter of Idemili. When Asala, the daughter of Edo, died, Edo divorced Eze Mewi and married Otoyogwe of Ichida. Eze Mewi ravaged the town of Ichida with a plague. After a great struggle, the two rivals made peace and Eze Mewi recovered his wife. To placate her and make her stay, he gave her a place of honour in the Nnewi pantheon.[24]

Many writers on Igbo religion have not distinguished between the deities, *mmuọ* and the Aṛusi. They discuss them all under the term *Aṛusi* and see no difference in their nature or rôles.[25] This has left many aspects of Igbo traditional religion very blurred. It is necessary here to emphasize and illustrate once again the point that there *is* an essential difference between the deities and the Aṛusi. The most obvious difference is that whereas the Aṛusi are the property of and are worshipped within the clan which owns them, the belief and worship of the deities like Anyanwụ, Ala, Agwụ, Chi and Ikenga are accepted by most Igbo groups. The second fundamental difference is that whereas the deities, like Ala, are fully personal and are therefore loving, merciful, just and kind, the Aṛusi are not fully rational and therefore sometimes act irrationally.

Although by their nature Aṛusi are good, they are very much feared because they can act blindly, though they follow their own rules which are basically just. This is reflected in ritual and the various uses to which Aṛusi are put. They can be invoked against one's enemies; they can also be invoked to protect properties against thieves, or for self-defence during journeys through enemy country. Some people bond themselves to serve one particular Aṛusi and derive great profit therefrom. But as we have observed, Aṛusi act like electric wires and vent their rage on whoever infringes their laws, even inadvertently. At Ihiala there is a forest still tabooed to an Arụsi in Okija called Ogwugwu-Mmili. The story has it that a woman from Okija, widow of an Ihiala man, had invoked the Arụsi on her husband's family because they had maltreated her. To vindicate her honour, the Arụsi wiped out the entire family, including her own sons. The whole property, now overgrown by forest, was tabooed to the spirit and has remained so.

If an Arụsi gets out of control and begins to kill indiscriminately, a powerful medicine-man may be invited to perform rites 'to tie the spirit': *ike ya*, or to chase it away. Rev. Basden reports how he was invited to drive away the Arụsi *Ngene*, which had become a hostile spirit in the vicinity. The villagers were certain about his ability to do this because 'Ngene could not exercise power over one who prayed to Chukwu'. This clearly bears out the theory of the hierarchy of being which we have enunciated. Chukwu is the first, most powerful being in the ontological hierarchy. A being in the Igbo ontology is not static but is in dynamic relationship with other beings. Its power can have beneficent or disruptive effects on other beings.

There are rites for restoring equilibrium in the ontological order by neutralizing the power of the being who is the source of the disruptive influence. Secondly, the belief and worship of Arụsi is the basis of what is sometimes called 'fetishism' and 'animism' in Igbo religion. The Igbo do not worship material objects, and what can be termed 'animism' in Igbo religion is restricted to the belief and worship of Arụsi. Both these conclusions are clearly borne out by the above analysis and by Basden's assessment of Ngene's power: 'When the spirit withdraws, or is driven out of a 'juju' the material and visible parts are no more valuable, or worthy of honour, than the shell of a nut after the kernel has been extracted.'[26]

Evil spirits

As there are hundreds of good spirits, there are also hundreds of evil spirits. Efforts to find a figure in the Igbo traditional world-view to represent the Christian concept of the Devil, has led to the identification of an Igbo deity,

Ekwensu, with the Christian Devil. In the Igbo translations of the Bible, in the catechisms and hymn books of various Christian churches, the Devil is translated and identified with Ekwensu. This has led many writers to represent Ekwensu in Igbo traditional religion as the arch-enemy of Chukwu and the supreme author of evil, 'whose one purpose is to frustrate the goodness of God and to disseminate evil'.[27] It is necessary to point out at once that this dualism does not exist in Igbo religion. Fr. Correia has warned that: 'Ekwensu, which is the name the Christians have adopted to translate the Devil, is an evil spirit which is feared because it is the spirit of somebody who died poor and without a family.'[28] This view, however, which identifies Ekwensu with the malignant dis-embodied spirits, is also a missionary accretion which has completely confused Christian and traditional Igbo beliefs.

The evil spirits to which Correia is referring are the *Akalogeli* or wandering spirits, those of people who died without children or wealth and have therefore received no funeral rites. Unable to reach the spirit-land they wander, restless and disgruntled, about the world, trying to make life unbearable for their surviving relations. *Ogbonuke*, 'dead contemporaries', is another class of evil spirits. They represent age-grade members who died young, frustrated because they have not been able to achieve 'the aim and purpose of their lives on earth', their *Akala Aka*. Now they mischievously try to bring misfortunes on their surviving comrades, with perhaps the hope that they too, in spite of a longer span of life, will not accomplish their *akala aka* – 'the destiny inscribed on their palms by the creator'.

There is also a group of evil spirits believed to be spirits of children. These *Ogbanje*, repeaters, are a terror to parents, for they are believed to be spirits of children who organize themselves in their pre-natal state into clubs, *Ndi otu*, to punish their parents by reincarnating in the same family several times, only to die in infancy each time. A woman infested by *ogbanje* may give birth up to nine times but may not have any surviving issue as they (or according to Igbo belief the same 'repeater') would die each time before adulthood. The aim of the *Ogbanje*, like the *Ogbonuke* and *Akalogeli*, is the same; to make the lives of the living useless

by preventing them from realizing their supreme purpose
– long life, many wives and children, and grand funeral
ceremonies to assure them of a place of honour in the
spirit-land.

It is therefore easy to see that the Igbo concept of evil
spirits does not include the idea of moral evil. Unlike the
Christian concept of the Devil and 'his angels' who are evil
because they incite people to immoral behaviour, Igbo evil
spirits do not incite people to immoral deeds but bring them
misfortunes.[29] They are essentially evil because they never
bring good fortune. Evil spirits are not worshipped but are
driven away by the rite of *Ichụ Aja*.

Ekwensu

Ekwensu is not the devil but an Arụsi. Its rôle differs among
different Igbo groups. However, it is generally regarded as
a spirit of violence by most Igbo as it incites people to
violence. This can be very useful during wars and Ekwensu
is therefore invoked by warriors and head-hunters. But
Ekwensu may also incite people to violence during
peacetime and the results may be disastrous. A person who
acts recklessly is asked *Ekwensu ọna-akpa gi?* 'Are you possessed by Ekwensu?' Violent deaths are called *Ọnwụ Ekwensu*.[30]
At the funeral ceremonies of warriors, their surviving comrades are supposed to do deeds of daring. They sometimes
run around singing, *'Onwe nwa kpọrụ nwa ya, na Ekwensu
abam n'anya'*, 'whoever has a child let him take him away,
because I am now possessed by Ekwensu'.

In many parts of Igboland, especially on the western side
of the Niger, there is an annual festival in honour of
Ekwensu called *Igba Ọsọ Ekwensu*, 'running for Ekwensu'.[31]
Warriors and all who have taken the title of *Ọgbụ Mmadụ*,
Man killer, parade the town glorying in their valour and
singing the praises of Ekwensu. Paradoxically the rituals
include purification rites and rites for driving away
Ekwensu, since its activities during peacetime would spell
disaster for the community.[32]

Uru Chi (destroyer of fortune)

The only non-human spirit which is regarded as essentially evil in the Igbo sense is *Uru Chi*. The name itself means 'destroyer of fortune'. Uru Chi strives to render null and void any favours Chi intends to send to her child, and strives to frustrate any requests and sacrifices offered to Chi by her child. Its activities are therefore completely negative. But here, as in the case of the disembodied evil spirits, there is a complete absence of any moral element in the conception and activities of Uru Chi. Evil spirits for the Igbo are those who bring misfortune. An informant explains the relationship between Chi and Uru Chi thus: 'Uru Chi is like a spoilt daughter of Chi. She takes delight in distracting worshippers of Chi and thwarting the gifts of fortune Chi sends to them'.[33]

This is expressed in ritual. A person may set up a shrine for Uru Chi, says Horton, only 'on the instruction of a diviner after a series of personal misfortunes which sacrifice to Chi has failed to avert'.[34] The shrine is set up at the left hand side of Chi's shrine but set back a little. Crumbs of whatever is given to Chi are also offered to Uru Chi, but this is done with the left hand and from behind one's back, while saying, *'Uru Chi were nke gi'*, 'Uru Chi take your own'. This underlines the evil nature of Uru Chi and emphasizes that the cult is more of an exorcism than worship.

Thus the Christian concept of a 'Devil' who is the arch-enemy of God, who takes delight in inciting men to moral evil so as to alienate them from Him, does not exist in Igbo religion. Akalogeli, Ọgbọnuke, Ọgbanje, and the nameless evil spirits are neither conceived as enemies of God nor do they incite people to moral evil. When Ekwensu, which like every other Arụsi is generally regarded as a good spirit, incites somebody to acts of violence resulting in bloodshed in his own community, it is regarded as a moral evil. Only Ekwensu, therefore, is believed to incite people to moral evil and only in this very restricted area; thus the notion of inciting people to moral evil enters the conception of Ekwensu and one can understand why the idea of Ekwensu as the 'tempter' or the 'devil' caught on easily with the Igbo. Today, among Igbo Christians and non-Christians alike, every evil deed is said to be *Ọru Ekwensu*, the work of the devil.

The rôle of divination and oracles

The Igbo world-view is overcrowded by spirits of all sorts, deities, Arụsi, evil spirits and so forth. The deities, *Mmụọ*, are indeed numerous, but they are few enough to be known to the ordinary Igbo believer. On the other hand, the Arụsi are so great in number that nobody is expected to know them all. Moreover, as new Arụsi and other powerful mystical forces are invented, old ones fade into oblivion. And yet any worshipper should be prepared to placate both the new and the old. This leaves a believer subject to constant fear because he does not know from where to expect the next problem. Because of the great numbers of these spirit-forces, and the fact that their spheres of influence and taboos so overlap, it takes an expert to know which spiritual force is responsible for any given misfortune and therefore which are the appropriate remedies to take. This enhances the rôles of the *dibia Afa*, diviner, and the oracles.

The diviner has the indispensable rôle of helping the sufferer to discover whether the said misfortune comes from human agents from within the community – witches or sorcerers – or from spiritual agents from outside – an evil spirit or an Arụsi. When this is established, the sufferer still needs the diviner to find out who or which particular spirit is responsible and what remedies to apply. This can be a source of great anxiety and might involve a worshipper in a considerable loss of time and resources. The accusation that, although the African recognizes God as Creator and Lord of all things, he allows his fear and concern for the deities elbow God into the background, may be justified by the concern and attention shown to the innumerable subordinate deities who crowd the African world-view.

Most believers would not embark on any important venture without first resorting to one form of divination or another. Options range from simple forms of divination which he can operate for himself, like throwing four pieces of kola on the ground and reading the meaning of the relationship between those pieces which fall face upwards and those which fall face downwards, to making a pilgrimage to the shrine of one of the oracles where Chukwu Himself is believed to reveal hidden things. In the eighteenth and nineteenth centuries, three of these oracles achieved great fame: the great Arochukwu oracle, Ibinokpabe (known to early explorers as long Juju), Igwekala, the oracle of Umunnoha, and Agbala, oracle of Awka. They were consulted by devotees from all over Igboland and neighbouring tribes in the belief that the Supreme God, Chukwu, manifested himself there and spoke directly to those who enquired.[35] The oracles therefore took on the attributes of the Supreme Being. The Arochukwu oracle took on the name Chukwu, and his praise-name *Ibinokpabe*, 'one who receives you kindly and fills your baskets.' *Eligwe wu anya Chukwu, Ala wu nti ya*, 'Heaven is the eye of Chukwu, the earth his ears'; He is *Okpo oku umu mmuo*, 'One who summons all the deities', *Onye okwu biri na onu ya*, the final arbiter. The Agbala oracle is called *Agbala Chukwu Okike*, 'Agbala, son of God the creator'. He is acclaimed as discerner of the secrets of men, the judge of poisoners, the revealer of witchcraft, the omnipotent one, the forgiver of sins, the dispenser of blessings of every kind, including the gift of children.[36] A common term for consulting an oracle is still *Ije Chukwu*, going to (consult) God.

Oracular institutions in Igboland have been described as a 'brilliantly organized system of deceit'. There is, in fact, much deceit, fraud and crimes being practised by the oracular agents and at the shrines. The belief in the omniscience of the oracles is sustained in most communities by a network of informants. Many pilgrims who visit the shrines are robbed, murdered, or sold into slavery. Of the Arochukwu oracle, for example, it is said that it used to reveal its oracles in a cave through which a stream flows. It gave its oracles in nasal tones in the dialect of the enquirer, thus giving the impression that Chukwu is universal and omniscient. Many pilgrims who entered the cave to consult it are said to have been led away through a secret passage and sold into slavery, while the blood of a goat was poured into the stream to convince the relatives that Chukwu had taken the enquirer's life. Igwekala and Agbala also give their oracles in a disguised voice in thick forests where it is easy to get rid of their victims. In January 1910, the British District commissioner, Mr. Chamley, raided a cave and caught two people in the act of impersonating the Chukwu oracle. A raid on the hideout of the Agbala oracle in 1921 resulted in the discovery of several blood-stained clubs and bodies with cracked skulls buried in shallow graves.

Nevertheless, as one Aro elder stated, 'the confidence of people continues to repose in them after they had been destroyed several times'[37] and this shows that they still cater for some vital religious and cultural need: oracles and divination are closely associated with God, the architect of man's fortune. Only He has the key to its secrets and can best advise how to get the best from one's fortune. Again, in Igbo societies which have no centralized authority, oracles serve as a final court of appeal, so the rôle of the oracle is indispensable in the Igbo world-view, in which deities, spirits and forces are numbered in hundreds. In many cases, the pronouncement of an oracle is necessary to indicate to the worshipper to which deity he should address himself and the appropriate rituals.

Conclusion

From the foregoing analysis it is evident that the deities are very closely associated with God. They are created by God and are subordinate to Him. They are His messengers. Their intimate but subordinate relationship with God is conceptualized in terms of father/son, chief/messenger, or lord/servant. Their status is not very different from that of angels in the Christian doctrine. In practice, however, acts of worship addressed to them seem to indicate that they act independently of God in bestowing their favours and inflicting punishments. The popular mind does not bother to define the limits of the deities' powers in relation to the supreme sovereignty of God, but they do know that the deities are creatures of God and derive their powers from God. In their spheres of influence, they may act independently, but God can always intervene when He wants and when He does, His will prevails. To ask whether African Traditional Religion is monotheistic or polytheistic is not a fair question; these concepts were evolved in another historical and cultural context and neither fits the African pattern.

The convenient solution has been to push African traditional religion into one or other of these moulds whether it fits or not. Some have called it monotheism, others have called it polytheism. Some are beginning to discover that it fits into neither category and have talked of 'diffused monotheism'. While the search for adequate terms continues, it is important to note as a practical conclusion that African religion believes in one God who is served by many divine beings. These divine beings are not *gods*, and should not be called such. In Igbo they are *Mmụọ*, spirits or deities, to differentiate them from the *Arụsi* spirit-forces.

Notes

1 Busia, K. A. 'The Ashanti', in *African Worlds*, ed. Forde, Daryll (1968), p.193.
2 Evans-Pritchard, E. E. *Nuer Religion* (1970) p.51.
3 Idowu, B. *Olodumare* (1962) p.62.
4 Alutu, J. O. *A Groundwork of Nnewi History* (1963). Cf. Arinze, F. A. *Sacrifice in Ibo Religion* (1970) p.25.
5 Okafor Awali Tape-recorded interview of an elder of Nnewi, Ofolo.
6 Meek, C. K. *Law and Authority in a Nigerian Tribe* (1937) p.22.
7 Horton, W. R. C. 'God, Man and Land in a Northern Ibo Village-Group', *Africa*, 26 (1956) p.21.
8 Interview with Ezeana Nwaezeako, the chief priest of Umudioka village, Awka.
9 Meek, C. K. op. cit. (1937) p.23.
10 Meek, C. K. ibid. p.22. Cf. Shelton, A. J. 'The Presence of the Withdrawn High God In North Ibo Religious Belief and Worship', *Man*, 65 (1965) p.15.
11 Uchendu, V. C. *The Igbo of Southeast Nigeria* (1965) p.9.

12 Anozia, I. P. 'The Religious Import of Igbo Names',
    unpublished thesis, Urban University, Rome (1968)
    p.32.
13 Ezeanya, S. M. in *Biblical Revelation and African Beliefs*,
    ed. Dickson, Kwesi A. and Ellingworth, P. (1969) p.37.
14 Meek, C. K. op. cit. (1937) p.24.
15 Anozia, I. P. op. cit. (1968) p.33.
16 Horton, W. R. C. op. cit. (1956) p.18.
17 Talbot, P. A. *The Peoples of Southern Nigeria* Vol.2,
    (1926) p.292.
18 Shelton, A. J. op. cit. (1965) p.18.
19 Nweke Ezeamalu Tape-recorded interview with an
    elder from Awba, Njikoka Divison.
20 Jeffreys, M. D. W. 'Ikenga – The ram-headed God'
    African Studies, Vol. 13, No. 1, (1965) p.40.
21 There is an Arụsi called *Akpu*, but this refers to the
    silk-cotton tree not the cassava tuber which is also called
    Akpu.
22 Alutu, J. O. op. cit. (1963) p.106.
23 Alutu, J. O. ibid. Apparently Arụsi may also die.
24 Basden, G. T. *Niger Ibos*, (1966). Cf. Uchendu, V. C.
    op. cit. All make no distinction between Arụsi and the
    deities.
25 Basden, G. T. op. cit. (1966) p.215.
26 Basden, G. T. ibid., pp.36–37.
27 Correia, Alves 'L'Animisme Ibo et les Divinités de la
    Nigéria', *Anthropos* (1922) p.365.
28 Any spirit whose name is unknown is potentially
    harmful and is best driven away by the rite of *Ichụ Aja*.
29 Noon, A. John 'A Preliminary examination of the
    death concept among the Ibo', *American Anthropologist*
    No. 44 (1944) p.640.
30 Crowther, S. and Taylor, J. *The Gospel on the Banks of
    the Niger* (1968 ed.) p.378.
31 Basden, G. T. op. cit. (1966) p.3. Cf. Isichei, E. 'Ibos
    and Christian Beliefs; some aspects of a theological
    encounter', *African Affairs*, 68 (1969) p.124.
32 Ezekwugo, C. 'Chi the true God in Igbo Religion'
    unpublished thesis, University of Innsbruck (1973)
    p.208. Gives an account of purification rites during the
    Ekwensu festival at Arochukwu.

33 Horton, W. R. C. op. cit. (1956) p.20.
34 Baikie, W. B. *Narrative of an Exploring Voyage up the Rivers, Kwora and Binue commonly known as the Niger and Tsadda in 1854* (London, 1856) p.313.
35 Basden, G. T. op. cit. (1966) p.84.
36 Isichei, E. op. cit. (1969) p.124.
37 Tape-recorded interview with Nwafor Okafor, an Aro Elder.

6 God, ancestors and man

The previous chapter examined the relationship between God and the non-human spirits. This chapter discusses the relationship between God and human spirits; these include spirits which once were human beings such as ancestral and reincarnated spirits, living human beings who possess certain supernatural powers – for example, witches, sorcerers – and, of course, man himself who, though visible, is regarded as a living spiritual being. First, an examination of the African concept of man:

Man

The African doctrine of man does not admit the dualism which is characteristic of the western Graeco-Roman culture. Man is not split into two conflicting principles, the body and the soul. African anthropologies generally conceive of man as one unit: there are indeed a number of principles in man, but these do not contradict his unity. They are, rather, principles which link man, 'the real person', with other beings in the ontological order. Some African anthropologies identify four principles in each man. There is the 'soul' conceived as a vivifying principle, a life-force which links man in a vital relationship with the other life-forces in the universe. There is the 'destiny soul', conceived of as an 'emanation' or 'spark' of the Creator, which, together with the Creator, assists man to realize his individual destiny. The ancestral spirit also believed to be incarnate in man links him with his family, clan and other human societies and finally there is the human being himself, usually called 'the real person', the unique individual created by God. The shadow is the visible representation of 'the real person' who is essentially invisible. Of course, different societies conceive of these principles and their relationships in different ways but the general conception of man as a unit and a life-force in vital relationship with other life-forces in the universe is a characteristic feature. The moral ideal is generally the same – a harmonious integration of the self with the world, and the most sinister beings – witches and sorcerers – are the avowed agents for the disruption of this harmony.

Ashanti

The Ashanti of Ghana believe that man has besides his *sunsum*, also a *kra*. A man's *sunsum* is his ego, his personality, his distinctive character. It is not divine, but perishes with the man. This personality-soul may wander about in sleep and be captured by witches. A man's *kra* on the other hand is a life-force, 'the small bit of the creator that lives in every person's body' and it returns to the creator when the person dies. Each person receives this spirit directly from God together with his destiny. From his father, man receives *Ntoro*, a spirit life-force which links him with his paternal lineage group or *Ntoro* group. Man is formed from the blood, *Mogya,* of the mother, and the spirit, *Ntoro,* of the father. Those who share the same blood belong to the matriclan.[1] The Ashanti are matrilineal, so they have cults only for the ancestors of their matriclan.

Yoruba

The Yoruba also believe that man has multiple souls. First there is the *Emi*, associated with breath. It resides in the lungs and chest and is man's vital force, his life principle. Man dies when *Emi* leaves the body: it may also leave the body during sleep and be trapped or eaten by witches. Witches can send their *Emi* to attack others. Then there is the *Iponri* or personal destiny. This is associated with the head, *Ori*,[2] and conceived of as a spirit-double. One part is in heaven and acts as a guardian-spirit: the other in a person's head and represents his destiny. The 'spirit-guardian in heaven' choses a person's *Ori* or destiny before he is born, kneeling before *Olodumare* the Creator who thereupon fixes it on the head. Thereafter the *Iponri* in heaven helps a person to realize his destiny on earth.[3] *Iponri*, also called *Eleda*, represents the partial rebirth or reincarnation of a patrilineal ancestor; so it is sometimes called the person's 'guardian ancestor'. Also associated with man is *Ojiji*, shadow, which follows him about but has no function.

Igbo

The Igbo doctrine of man believes that man is a creature of God, *Ekechukwu*, not only because the first human pair was sent down by God from heaven, but because it is also believed that God creates each individual person. Four constituent principles can be distinguished in man: *Obi*, heart or breath, *Mmuo* (sometimes called *Onyinyo*), spirit or shadow, *Chi*, destiny, and *Eke*, personality or ancestral guardian. The heart, *Obi*, is man's life-force and links him with the cosmic force. The spirit, *Mmuo*, is 'the real self' directly created by the Creator. The destiny-spirit, *Chi*, is a spark of the creator in man which assigns to each his personal destiny, while the ancestral guardian, *Eke*, links man to his clan life-force.

Obi (breath or heart)

Obi – heart or breath – is man's animating principle and the seat of affection and volition. For example, a good and kindly man is called *Onye obi oma* and a courageous man is called *Onye obi ike*. *Obi*, breath, resides in the biological heart which is also called *Obi*, but the 'breath' is an immaterial spiritual substance which sometimes leaves the body – in dreams and under the influence of witchcraft. Of the fright or sensation one feels in the face of sudden danger, the Igbo say *Obi'm efepu*, 'My heart has flown away'. The breath is a life force which links man with other cosmic forces. It may be attacked through witchcraft or sorcery and may be weakened or die. It can be strengthened by magic or by eating another human heart through witchcraft or ritual cannibalism. At death, the heart leaves the body but it does not survive.[4] Nowadays, one often hears of *mkpulobi*, seed of the heart; it is becoming customary to translate *mkpulobi* as 'soul' and identify it with the Christian soul, but this is a concept completely alien to traditional Igbo beliefs. Traditionally, *mkpulobi* is the same as *Obi*, breath, as defined above.

Chi (destiny)

Chi is believed to be an emanation of the Creator, a spark of Him in each person. It is conceived of as a spirit double, one resident in heaven; the other in the individual. In this sense it may be said to be the practical application of the Divine Providence to each person. When a man dies, his Chi goes back to God to give account of his work and conduct. Women have cults for Chi. After the birth of their first baby, they set up their own shrines with relics taken from their mother's shrines. Men invoke Chi, but do not establish cults. (See chapter 2 for fuller treatment of the Chi concept.)

Eke (ancestral guardian)

Eke is believed to be an ancestral shade incarnate in each newly born baby. *Eke* is therefore connected with the Igbo concept of reincarnation. A person's Eke is usually referred to as *Onye noro ya uwa* 'the person who brought him to the world' and is usually an ancestor, a deity or an Arusi. The child is believed to take after the *onye noro ya uwa* in appearance or in character. In cases of doubt, the parents consult a *dibia* or diviner and perform the rites of *Igba Agu*. If this is not done, the child may fall sick and die because the parents cannot identify the person who has been reincarnated, nor be certain of the taboos and cults he must observe. Eke links the individual with the life-force of his patriclan. The belief in Eke makes it possible for the dead to reincarnate in the living from generation to generation.

Each person makes sacrifices to his Eke for good fortune. As soon as the diviner identifies the Eke the parents arrange to perform the rites of bringing the *Eke* to their home. This is done by the eldest male. He takes kola nuts to the grave of the appropriate deceased relative and in a simple prayer asks the *Eke* to follow him home. He touches the place with a knotted palm frond, carries it home and places it in the family *onu okike* or shrine to Eke. After a sacrifice, the *Eke* is believed to have come home.[5]

Mmuo or Onyinyo (spirit or shadow)

What survives after death is *Mmuo*, the spirit. *Mmuo* – unlike the Christian concept of a soul as a spirit separated from the body – is not a *part* of man, but the full, real person, '*onye ahu*'. During a man's lifetime and after his death, *mmuo* is imagined as being like the shadow cast by the human body and is therefore sometimes called *Onyinyo*, shadow. The *Onyinyo* of an adult is like a fully grown man; that of a baby is like a baby. The belief appears to be that *Mmuo* is directly created by God and pre-exists its appearance in the human form. Many of these pre-natal human beings include the spirits, *mmuo*, of dead children and men who died in youth. Each person is believed to have received a definite assign-ment from God to be accomplished during his term of life on earth. If prevented by an untimely death, then he must reincarnate to finish it. The belief inspires such expressions as *Arusibeghi m ihe m'biara n'elu uwa*, 'I have not accomp-lished what I came into the world for'. Spirits of children and dead youths are believed to be floating in the air, looking for an opportunity to reincarnate. The belief in the pre-natal human existence is effectively borne out by the Igbo belief in *Ogbanje* – repeaters (*Abiku* – born to die): see page 76.

The creation of the human shadow is therefore the pre-rogative of Chukwu. God is equally involved in the second stage in the process of bringing human beings to life, when the *mmuọ* goes before Chukwu to receive his *Chi* and *Eke*, his destiny and personality and then *Eke* brings him into the world, '*inọ ụwa*'. This Igbo concept of reincarnation may be described as partial reincarnation. The spirit or *mmuọ* of the Eke remains an ancestor in the spirit-land; only his personality representing the life force of his family is passed on to the newly born child who also retains his own spirit, *mmuọ*, the real man. One often hears people say what they would like to be in their next life cycle. A woman may wish to be a man and poor people may wish to be rich.

Ancestors

This doctrine of reincarnation implies that the life of man extends beyond his sojourn in this world and includes the after life and the pre-natal state. Life is an interminable cycle of birth, death and rebirth. The same spirit, '*Mmuọ*', the real person, passes through the three stages and reincarnates again (at least partly) to continue the process. However, *Mmuọ* attains full maturity and status when it becomes an ancestor. Passage from one stage of existence to another is marked by rites of passage. Of these the most important are the 'birth rites', the 'puberty rites' and finally the 'burial rites' which usher the person home to the *Ala Mmuọ*, or spirit-land where he takes his place among the Ancestors. So one finds that the three rites of passage form a linked process by which the 'spirit', *mmuọ*, acquires its full 'ancestor' status.

The rites of passage

The birth rites separate the spirit of a child from the pre-natal world and integrate him into the society of the living. In the Okigwe area, this ceremony is called *Ihuja Nwata*, 'frightening the child'. It is believed that until this ceremony is performed, the child is not interested in the society of men – it still communicates with its comrades in the pre-natal world and takes an active part in the activities of its age-group there. As part of the rites, children of four and under are left in a room with the baby, then they are taken out of the room and made to rush in again and all shout at the baby at once. This attracts the attention of the baby away from the non-human group to the human community.[6]

Puberty rites for boys are called *Ima mmụọ*, knowing the spirits. In this context the spirits are ancestors and this is the initiation into the secret society of masked men. To the uninitiated, the masqueraders are ancestors who have temporarily come back in visible form to participate in the affairs of the family of which they still are active members. In many Igbo societies laws are still promulgated and enforced by masqueraders who, as ancestors, are held to be custodians of customs and traditions. On initiation day, the masqueraders collect the initiates from the village and disappear with them into the forest where their shrine is located. There, they are subjected to many hardships to teach them endurance, and are taught the secret codes of the *mmụọ* society. Finally, they are shown that the *mmụọ* are, in fact, relations of theirs who have been wearing masks. Finally, they are placed under oath never to reveal the secrets of the rite. Meanwhile, the uninitiated are made to believe that at the shrine, the masqueraders swallow them, and take them down to the spirit-land where they learn the secret language and share the knowledge of the ancestors.

The funeral rites make the spirits of the dead reach the spirit-land. Death alone does not make an ancestor; appropriate funeral rites must introduce him to the presence of God. If God approves of his life on earth, he becomes an ancestor, *Ndichie*. If not, he is banished to *Ama Nri Mmụọ na Mmadụ*, an intermediate state between the human world and the spirit-world.[7]

After the funeral rites, shrines are set up in honour of ancestors inside the reception hut, *Obi*. At Owerri an ancestral shrine consists of a wooden pillar about one foot thick and one-and-a-half feet wide. It is placed inside the hut facing out so that the ancestor can see what is happening outside. Behind the pillar is a wooden panel with openings 'to give eyes to the ancestors'. The most important symbol of the ancestors is *Ọfọ*, a small branch of the *Ọfọ* tree (*Detarium Senegalense*). This is believed to have been set aside by Chukwu as a symbol of authority.[8] An inherited

Ọfọ becomes a symbol of inherited authority. The lineage Ọfọ is the outward symbol of the presence of the ancestors and must therefore be displayed when the living are assembled for important family discussions. In very serious and controversial issues which could threaten the peace and solidarity of the clan, the Ọkpala or head of the family may decide to impose a decision with the Ọfọ, in which case, he may hit the ground four times with it and say, 'Anyone who disobeys this decision, may this Ọfọ kill him', and all present respond simultaneously Ihaa 'Let it be so'.[9]

The African ancestral cult

The cult Africans give to their glorified dead has often been described as 'ancestor worship', but many find this term inadequate. Driberg, for example, has argued that 'no African prays to his dead grandfather any more than he prays to his living father'.[10] If it is accepted that worship is an expression of one's submission and dependence on a supernatural spiritual being, it is difficult to see why this term should not be applied to the cult given to ancestors. There is apparently very little difference between the cult given to the deities and that given to the ancestors. Both are given offerings of food and fresh blood, the form of the prayers are similar, and the attitude of the worshippers shows very little difference. In some prayers and sacrifices, ancestors are invoked along with the Supreme Being and the deities. Much therefore depends on the African belief in the nature of the ancestors' powers in relation to God on the one hand, and to man on the other. Do Africans approach the ancestors as the ultimate source of the powers which they exercise over them, or are they merely intermediaries? If they are merely intermediaries, any worship given to them would not be for their own sakes but in recognition of the vital rôle they play. The term Dulia which Catholic theology uses to describe the worship given to saints, in contrast to Latria, the worship given to God, has been suggested as a suitable term with which to describe the African ancestral cult.[11]

Plate 6 Masks are believed to be ancestors visiting the living in visible forms

Nevertheless in many African societies, even though the ancestors acquire greater powers which put them next to the deities in the ontological order so that they become mediators between God and man, yet they are still members of their families, and are best called the 'living dead' as Mbiti suggested. Consequently, the living approach them in the same way as they did when they were alive. The respect given them is often incongruously mixed with the casual manners of a normal family gathering. They are approached as comrades and elder kinsmen who have as much interest in the welfare of the family as their living kinsmen. The form of the prayers is direct, the requests are straightforward – as if to say that it is also in their interest to grant them. The tone of submission and supplication which appears in prayers to God and the deities is significantly absent. They may be rebuked, insulted or even threatened.

Tempels has pointed out that the Bantu (who have no well-organized pantheon of deities) recognize an essential difference in the veneration of founders of the clan and lineages and the ordinary ancestors. With the former who are so near God that they are called *ba-vidye*, spiritual beings, 'there can be no pact or contractual relationship, they must not be scorned; no reproaching when disasters occur, only filial subjection can re-establish alignment with the vital force of the forebears, while the recently dead, who were known during their lifetime are regarded as equals.'[12] In West Africa, where there are huge pantheons of deities, ancestors who attain the status of deity, like *Shongo*, do so by usurping the position of an earlier deity.

The Igbo ancestral cult

Offerings made to the ancestors are called by the Igbo *inye fa nni*, feeding them. Ancestors may be persuaded to grant a request by promises of a more generous offering or by a threat of starving them should they fail. Sometimes the relationship with the ancestors is believed to be governed by the principle of reciprocity. The Igbo say, *'Aga na achu aja, ka ikpe na ama ndi mmuo'*, 'We shall continue to make offerings so that the fault will lie with the ancestors'.

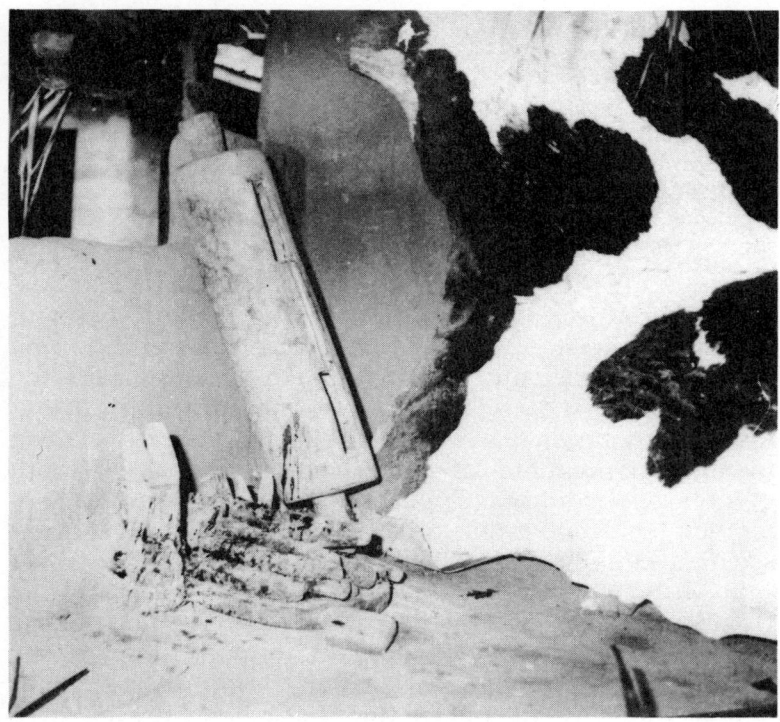

Plate 7 An ancestral shrine in the Obi (reception hut). Notice the stain of blood offerings on the Ikenga, and the Ọfọ

This notwithstanding, the Igbo are very close to their ancestors. They receive more attention in daily and annual acts of worship than the Supreme Being or the deities. As members of the family they are invited to be present and participate in most family activities; they are invoked to share in the kola communion, whether it is blessed at public gatherings or split at home to entertain a guest. They are invoked to participate at naming ceremonies, marriages and funeral rites of other members of their family.

The Igbo morning offering, *Igọ Ọfọ*, 'praying with the "*Ọfọ*" ' is addressed to God, the deities and ancestors, but it is made before the ancestral shrine *Okpensi*. Kola, palmwine and phallic chalk, *nzu*, are offered to them. Occasionally, especially during their annual festivals or when directed by a diviner, offerings are made exclusively to the ancestors in the following manner:

First, there must be the customary washing of hands, followed by the offering of kola-nuts. Then the suppliant holds a fowl in both hands and, standing before the *Okpensi* says, 'Look, my father, you see this fowl, and you see these my children, and you know all about us. Please see that no harm befalls us, and deliver us from the evil designs of evil spirits and protect us well.'[13]

The annual festival of *Ilọ Mmụọ* 'feasting the spirits' is a time of family reunion and the strengthening of family ties with the ancestors. The *Ụmụ ada*, daughters of the lineage who have been married out, bring with them offerings which the *Ọkpala*, the head of the family, who is also the family priest, will offer to the ancestors on their behalf. Quarrels between members of the family are settled and the festival ends with great feasting and rejoicing. In his quarterly report of September 1869, Reverend Smart, a C.M.S. agent reported seeing a family meeting held at the ancestors' grave in an Igbo settlement in Bonny. They believed that the ancestors would preside over their meeting and settle their differences. 'This shed,' they explained to him, 'is the place the founder of this our village was buried, and so we are his people, and we come before him that he may preside over our palaver.'[14] The ancestors are thus symbols of peace, unity and prosperity in the family. At the same time, as protectors of traditional laws and customs, *Omenani* and the welfare of their families, the ancestors may punish any offenders. Sometimes, ancestors might even demand the death of a member of their family whose conduct threatens its survival. According to an informant, Ikwue Anikwue: 'Sometimes when a person is seriously sick he is said to be pleading his case before God and Ajana – *Ọnọ ikpe be Chukwu na Ajana*. His accusers are the ancestors. If he recovers he is said to have won his case against his accusers. Hence during such sickness he will be calling on the ancestors to leave him alone.'[15]

From Anikwue's words it would seem that the Ndichie have no rights over the life of the living. If so, the right to take away the life of the penitent is seen as the prerogative of *Chukwu*, God, and *Ajana*, Earth Deity. The Ndichie therefore content themselves with accusing him before God and the Earth Deity and asking for his death. This is intriguing evidence of how the Igbo organize the beings in their world-view: the Ala, the Ọfọ, Ndichie and men, under Chukwu, the Almighty Creator and Providence.

Other forces in the Igbo world-view

Besides Chukwu, the deities, Arụsi, Ndichie, and the evil spirits, there are two other mystical forces which feature prominently in the lives of the Igbo. These are *Ọgwụ*, medicines and *Amusu*, witchcraft. These forces are not spirit-forces; they live in the world of man and are completely within the control of man, but whereas *Ọgwụ* can be used for good or for evil, *Amusu* is always used for evil ends.

Ọgwụ (medicine)

The Igbo have a firm belief in the power of medicine, *Ọgwụ*. Making medicine is called *Igwọ Ọgwụ*. This same term translates the making of every kind of medicine, whether curative, protective, medicine made to secure good luck, or offensive medicine. However, the term *Ikọ Nsi*, sorcery or making bad medicine, is used to distinguish the evil use of medicines from its good uses. The specialist in the making of medicine is called *Dibia Ọgwụ* or medicine-man.

All medicines are made from herbs, hence the Igbo proverb: '*Ọgwụ agwụ n'ofia, afifia na akụ ọgwụ*', 'Medicine in the bush can never be exhausted, because medicine is extracted from herbs'. Different herbs produce different medicines and successful Igbo herbalists can cure many bodily ailments by their use. Some medicinal herbs, for example, those for the cure of malaria, snake bites and convulsions are commonly known. But the medicine prepared by a *dibia* is more powerful not only because he is an expert, but because he is in possession of *Agwụnsi*, a deity for medicine, whom he can invoke to give power to his medicine. So Ọgwụ is not just herbs; it must be charged with spiritual power by the use of rites, spells, and invocations.

Thus processed Ọgwụ can be made to serve any need.

Some are made to bring good luck. The famous Ọgwụ, 'ite awele' or pot of fortune, is said to bring quick and profitable sales to traders. It consists of a liquid made from herbs and other materials in which the owner washes his face every morning before he goes to market. Runaway wives, or relatives who have refused to return home can be brought home through using a special medicine. Some medicines are kept in portable materials to be carried about as charms. There is the famous charm Ebube Agụ na Eche agụ, 'the dignity of a lion protects the lion'. This is said to be made with the hair of a lion, and is supposed to make a person feared, esteemed and respected in public gatherings. It is therefore popular among politicians.

It is a pity that Christianity has indiscriminately condemned most African medicines as evil and diabolical magic. The Igbo have a different view. They would argue that Ọgwụ basically come from herbs; making medicine is only tapping the power which God put into things. It is African science and follows its own laws. For example, they will refer to a famous electric tree called Anụnụ ebe, literally 'a bird cannot perch'; as the name implies, it kills any living thing that comes in contact with it. But by some means, the Igbo collect it and transform it into very powerful protective and offensive medicines. This, they say, proves that Ọgwụ is science.

Nko Nsi (sorcery)

Unfortunately in some cases, people choose to transform the power of herbs, which God has put at the disposal of men, to wicked, evil purposes. The Igbo say: 'Ajọ mmadụ bụ ajọ mmụọ', 'An evil person is an evil spirit'. Among the most feared evil people in the community are ndi n'akpa nsi or ndi na agwọ ajọ ọgwụ; both terms mean sorcerers, evil men who make medicine to hurt others.

There are many ways of hurting others by 'bad' medicine. Hence the Igbo saying: 'ka asi si akọna nsi asi si efena ajụ', 'the law which forbids poisoning others does not mean that you may not cause them at least some dizziness'. The effect of ife ajụ lasts for some hours. A sorcerer may hurt a person by ikọ

Plate 8 Private shrine of Agwụ (Deity of Divination)

nsi, administering some poisonous concoction secretly hidden in his food, drink, or spread in the air which he breathes, or left in his farm or house to affect him by some form of contact.

Sorcery may also be practised through contagious magic. Objects which have had contact with the victim and are believed to be extensions of his personality, for example, his hair, nails or clothing, are ritually destroyed or mutilated. Such an act, it is believed, harms the intended victim. An informant told me that the Igbo do not practise purely sympathetic magic. You cannot harm a person by simply harming his image or an object which looks like him. He told me that even to make medicine to restrain a dead person's troublesome ghost at least some sand from his grave is required. However, other informants tell me that sympathetic magic is generally practised.

Sorcerers are very much feared and people take care to avoid them and are careful not to eat or drink anything in a sorcerer's home. The presence of a suspected sorcerer at public meetings makes everybody uneasy. A brief exchange of words with a sorcerer may make him begin to plan how to use his nefarious art on his opponent, but the community deals very severely with proven cases of sorcery. In some cases sorcerers are publicly executed. A suspect is subjected to a rigorous ordeal to prove his innocence. He may be forced to drink a poisonous concoction, to swear on a very dangerous Arụsi or, as happens in most cases, to drink the water used to wash the corpse of his victim. Very wicked sorcerers are forced by Ala to confess their crimes on their death-beds. This is called *isa n'ọnụ*, or forced confession. Such people are not buried; they are thrown into *Ajọ ọhia*, the bad bush.

Amusu (witchcraft)

Witches are clearly distinguished from sorcerers. The former are called *ndi amusu*, while the latter are called *ndi na akpa nsi*, 'those who deal in destructive medicine'. Belief in witchcraft is not found in all Igbo communities, but it is very strong among the riverside Igbo, *ndi olu*.

Igbo beliefs about witchcraft generally follow the African patterns already known in social anthropology. The woman is the witch, *Amusu*. Men who practise witchcraft are hard to find, but they do exist and are called *Ajalagba*, wizards. *Ajalagba* are by far more powerful and more dangerous than witches, hence the saying: *Amusu ada ebu ajalagba*, 'A witch cannot carry a wizard'. This has overtones of male chauvinism and is often used by men to remind women who appear to be very forward of their subordinate place in society.

A witch is a person who possesses a special psychic quality which permits her spirit, *Obi*, to leave her body, *arụ*, while she is asleep to afflict injuries on others or even to eat their souls. A witch uses no medicines, utters no spells and performs no rites. Her powers are inherent in her personality; she did not have to learn it like learning a trade. In this, it differs from *Igwọ Ọgwụ*, making medicine, or *Ikpa Nsi*, sorcery, which are arts and trades sometimes learnt through a long period of apprenticeship. Both witchcraft and sorcery have the same purpose, namely, the evil and devilish intention of injuring their fellow men by occult means. Some people are born witches, though witchcraft can also be acquired by swallowing a chemical substance inducing a psychic state which makes it possible for witches to leave their bodies and attack others spiritually. This will become more evident if we examine the process of acquiring witchcraft.

Witchcraft itself consists of two powers; the power of *eriri*, metempsychosis – of leaving one's body and changing to other forms, and the destructive mystical power of injuring others or eating their *Obi* or souls. Not everybody who has the power of *eriri* is a witch. There is ordinary *eriri* and there is *eriri Amusu*, witchcraft metempsychosis, so that every *Amusu* acquires the power of *eriri* in one of three ways. An introvert who is always internalizing grievances and conflicts and brooding over them, *Onye n'ebu ihe n'obi*, will soon discover that her soul begins to leave her body during sleep. She may quickly fall a prey to the witches who will invite her to join their club of soul-eaters. She becomes a witch as soon as she commits herself to do so. The powers of *eriri* can also be acquired by swallowing a chemical substance. Sorcerers give it to unsuspecting victims concealed in a banana fruit. Finally, a person may become a witch by exchanging saliva with a witch. The effect is always the same. The victim acquires the powers of a wandering soul with the added urge to hurt others, but she does not begin to exercise this unnatural urge until she commits herself to joining a witch club.

Witches attack their victims in several ways. They may carry away his soul to be shared at their nocturnal meetings. The victim wakes up weak and sick and dies as soon as they eat his soul. A wizard, *Ajalagba*, kills by smothering a victim, falling on him and trying to stop his breath with his crushing weight. Hence a wizard is sometimes called *Amusu ọdagbu*, 'a witch-killer by falling upon'. A witch may decide not to kill but to punish an enemy by inflicting serious injuries on him. She may cause blindness by spitting into the victim's eyes, or barrenness by tying up a victim's womb. A young girl whom I know had a sore on her foot which refused to heal after several years of treatment. People in the village still say that this was because a witch spat into her sore. Witches may destroy an enemy's crops or property.

The Igbo say that *Amusu adaghi ebu n'iro*, 'a witch never attacks an outsider'. The victim must be a close relation, a friend or a neighbour. The belief is that before a witch carries away a person's soul, she enters into spiritual communication with it, so it is only those whom she knows well enough to communicate with *ndi ọma obi ha*, that can become her victims. The second reason is based on the belief that the witch is sometimes forced to contribute her own children, her relatives, or even part of herself, to the ghoulish feast of the witch club, when she cannot find other victims. Hence witches are rarely healthy or happy and can be easily detected by relatives and neighbours. An introvert, a non-social person, a barren old woman, a wicked boastful person, is usually suspect.

Remedies for witchcraft are many and easily available. The commonest is a simple cocoyam tuber which is believed to be a taboo to witches. A cocoyam put under the pillow drives away a witch. A charm prepared by a *dibia* can catch a witch red-handed in her transformed form. Some Arụsi are known to be terrors to witches. Those dedicated to their service are never attacked by witches.

Once a person's soul has been shared by the witches, there is no remedy, but since this may be deferred, quick action after an attack may save a victim, but the co-operation of the witch is absolutely necessary to obtain the release of the soul of her victim. It involves a simple rite. The suspect witch cleans her mouth with water *Igbucha ọnụ*, and gives the victim a concoction made from herbs mixed with juice squeezed out of banana roots. If her gesture is genuine, the victim will recover. Many witches confess their evil deeds spontaneously or under torture or threat of being subjected to an ordeal. Others are identified by diviners or oracles. Witches, like sorcerers, are forced by Ala, the Earth Deity, to confess their crimes on their death-bed. Witches are not given funeral rites, their bodies are also thrown into *Ajọ ọhia*.

The synthesis of the rôle of God in the Igbo world-view

While trying to solve the puzzle of the multiplicity of spritual beings in the African world-view, many writers base their explanation solely on the fact that the African traditional world-view is anthropocentric, but make little of the fact that the same traditional world-view sees God as the principal source and end of the universe. Man is indeed at the centre of the universe. Above man is the Supreme Being and the ring of many and very powerful heavenly deities, while below him is Ala, Earth Deity, the queen of the underworld, presiding over hundreds of Aṛusi, local spirits and Ndichie, ancestors. In the ontological order of beings, man is in the centre, with God, the Deities, the Aṛusi and Ndichie above him, and the natural forces like Amusu, witchcraft, and Ọgwụ, medicine, below. Man looks to the superior divine forces for help and protection against evil spirits and the forces of evil, while he harnesses the lower forces in nature for his own fulfilment and the achievement of his goals in life.

But the above analysis of the Igbo world-view brings out the equally important fact that God is the 'Principal Source and End' of the universe. Everything in the universe comes from God, is continuously linked with God, is sustained by God, and tends towards God as its final end. This affirmation is true of both the spiritual beings and man. The Deities are creatures of God, subordinate beings to him and have been given different assignments by God. Ala, for example, is custodian of morality and traditional customs, Anyanwụ brings good fortune and Chi brings fertility.

Similarly, man comes from God and goes back to God. Man's life goes in a cycle. He comes from God into the world, and having fulfilled his mission in the world, *Akala Aka*, he goes back to God. If he realizes his *Akala Aka* in each case, God will bless him with an even more prosperous and happier term of life, and the cycle continues indefinitely. If he fails, the cycle is interrupted and he is banished to *Ama-nri-mmuọ na mmadụ*, an intermediate state between the human world and spirit world.

Notes

1 Busia, K. A. 'The Ashanti' in *African Worlds*, ed. Forde, Daryll (1968), p.196 ff.
2 Bascom, W. *Ifa Divination: Communication Between Gods and Men in West Africa* (1969) p.113.
3 Idowu, B. *Olodumare: God In Yoruba Belief* (1962) p.171.
4 Basden, G. T. *Niger Ibos* (1966) p.283.
5 Ezekwugo, C. 'Chi, the True God in Igbo Religion', Unpublished thesis, University of Innsbruck (1973) p.234.
6 Nwokocha, C. A. 'The Kola: Igbo Symbol of Love and Unity', Unpublished thesis, Urban University, Rome (1969) p.124 quoting Daly, J. *AFER*, IV (3 July 1964) p.262.
7 Leonard, A. G. *The Lower Niger and Its Tribes* (1968 ed.) p.141; cf. Basden, G. T., op. cit. (1966) p.286.
8 Meek, C. K. *Law and Authority In a Nigerian Tribe* (1937) p.63.
9 Ilogu, E. 'Ofo: A Religious and Political Symbol', *Nigerian Magazine* (Sept. 1964) p.234.
10 Driberg, J. H. in Supplement to *Journal of the Royal African Society* (Jan. 1936) Vol. 35, No. 138, quoted by Smith, E. W. *African Ideas of God* (1961) p.21.
11 Parrinder, E. G. *African Traditional Religion* (1954) p.65.
12 Tempels, Placide, *Bantu Philosophy* (1969) p.156
13 Basden, G. T. op. cit. (1966) p.284.
14 CA3/035/7 Niger Missions, 'Journal Excerpts' by W. Smart (Bonny, 1868–76).
15 Tape-recorded interview of Ikwue Anikwue, elder of Amanuke, Awka Division. Ajana is the local name for Ala (earth-deity).

7 God and morality

Myths about the origin of evil in the world, as examined in the first chapter, give us a clue to the relationship between God and morality. God is not responsible for the presence of evil in the world; He is given credit for all the good that there is in the world and the presence of evil is blamed on the irresponsible behaviour of a vulture. In the myth about the coming of death, the irresponsibility of the dog and the jealousy of the toad brought death into the world. The natural inference from these myths is that God, the Creator, is all good. Moreover, He requires moral goodness from his creatures. The myths distinguish between physical evils and moral evils; physical evils are punishment for moral evils; good fortune is the fruit of moral goodness, just as evil is the fruit of moral evil. This is a fundamental dogma in African ethical beliefs.[1]

The existence of moral consciousness in the African traditional religion can further be shown by analysing more of the terms, sayings, stories and practices which illustrate conscience, moral values and the moral code in African traditions. Some Africans believe that moral conscience is innate in man although this is not a logically reasoned philosophical conclusion, but more of a simple affirmation of belief which has grown out of the experience of life. Like the Yoruba, most Africans believe that:

'In order to aid man in ethical living, *Olodumare* has put in him *Ifa aya*, 'The oracle of the heart' or 'The oracle which is in the heart'. It is this oracle of the heart that guides man and determines his ethical life.'[2]

The Igbo are also aware of this small voice in man which directs him to good deeds and warns him of evil. They believe this voice comes from the heart, hence the Igbo word for conscience is *Obi*, heart. A good conscience is *Obi ọchā*, a clean heart and bad conscience is *Ajọ Obi*, a bad heart. The normal state of a man's conscience affects his character. A wicked man is called *Onye Ajọ obi*, a person with a bad heart, whereas a good and kindly person is called *Onye Obi ọma*. To express remorse, they say: '*Obi ya na apia ya itari*', 'His heart is flogging him'. The Igbo are very conscious of the necessity of having a good conscience, for God punishes those with a bad conscience. Hence the examination of conscience forms part of the Igbo daily morning prayer to God. Here is part of the morning prayer offered to God by an elder of Akum, a northern Igbo group. Addressing God by the title-name they use, he said:

Ezechitoke!	Lord, King, Creator!
Ọbụlụ na ni gbụlụ mmadụ	If I killed any person
Ọbụlụ na m tụtụlụ ife onye ọzọ	If I took another's property
Ọbụlụ na m gbalụ ama	If I bore false witness
Ọbụlụ na m bọlụ ji mmadụ	If I dug up another's yam
Ọbụlụ na m yili ọyi	If I committed adultery
Mọbụ nalụ mmadụ nwunye ya	Or abducted another's wife
Ezechitoke welụ ndum tata	Ezechitoke, take my life today.[3]

This sounds like a pharisaical prayer of self-glorification and in a sense it is. Igbo morality is linked with the ontological order set up by God and any infringement of the moral precepts disturbs the ontological order. The balance must then be restored by appropriate rituals, otherwise punishment will inevitably follow. This belief gives Igbo morality a legalistic outlook. Before engaging in any ritual, a man has to make sure of his ritual fitness to avoid further provoking an already offended deity. Sin is conceived primarily – though not exclusively – as an infringement of the natural law. Sin also includes the idea of an offence against a deity and a sense of the distortion of the moral rectitude which should exist in man.

The African moral code, unlike the Ten Commandments, is not written down. Rather it is preserved in oral tradition and forms part of the education given to its members by the traditional society. Its observance is a moral as well as a religious obligation. As in many preliterate societies, proverbs, names, sayings and folktales are not merely instruments for preserving moral ideals, but are very effective methods of teaching them. Many Igbo proverbs and sayings praise virtue and condemn vice; they approve of religion and disapprove of irreligion; they predict blessings for goodness and warn of the evil consequences of bad behaviour. An Igbo proverb warns the irreligious, *Mmadụ adaghi ekwe Chi mgba*, 'Nobody can wrestle with his God'.

Sin, punishment, and forgiveness also feature in Igbo proverbs: *Isi kote ebu, ya gbaba ya*, 'The head that disturbs a wasp, let it take the sting'; *Aduọ nti ọnụgh, ebiri isi ebiri nti*, 'When the ears will not listen to advice, when the head is cut, the ears fall with it'; *Mmehie adghi mgbaghara agaghi adi*, 'If there were no offences, there would be no forgiveness'; *Usa gwụ onye ọchụ n'ọnu, ọbia nwere ohiho*, 'When a murderer has exhausted his excuses, he finally hangs himself'. This tells of the Igbo practice which expects any murderer to hang himself honourably. These proverbs are ethical principles rather than categorical imperatives, but they bear out the fact that traditional ethics go beyond mere utilitarianism and the need to forge group solidarity.

Folktales, *akiko ifo*, were traditionally a very effective means of instructing the young. Informal story-telling sessions took place during moonlit games, and the children would sit, fascinated, for long hours around an elderly person and listen to thrilling tales. It was a leisure activity as well as a learning exercise. Most of the folktales have moralistic themes and tell how the trials and sufferings of the virtuous are finally rewarded and how the irreligious, the proud and the wicked are punished. Most Igbo children learn of God's omnipotence and man's total dependence on him in the famous story of a legendary wrestler *Ojadiri*, who won his fight against all mortals and all the spirits then, carried away by pride, challenged his Chi, or guardian spirit. His Chi threw him down with the tip of his finger, hence a person who wants to attempt the impossible is asked *Ina achọ igba Chi gi mgba*, 'Do you want to wrestle with your God?'

Another folktale portrays the evil consequences of jealousy and cupidity. It tells the story of the meeting of a rich man who possessed every imaginable luxury with a poor man who had only a bird which laid one golden egg every day. He made his living by selling this egg. Jealousy and avarice drove the rich man to plan the poor man's death by tempting him to a sumptuous banquet which he poisoned because he wanted the poor man's bird. The poor man succumbed to this temptation and the rich man got the bird. Driven by avarice, he killed the bird to get at all the gold that must be in its stomach – only to be disappointed.

The basis of African morality

Some anthropologists hold that the traditional moral law of the African can be traced not to an interior divine law but to the common good of the group. In this sense, the idea of sin does not exist for him outside the notion of injury to the community or mere personal selfish interests.

Correia, for example, credits the Igbo with the lowest form of moral consciousness. *'Le moral indigène est de l'utilitarisme au sens le plus vulgaire et le plus grossier.'*[4] 'The native sense of morality is of the lowest and most vulgar type of utilitarianism'! In support of this view, Margaret Field tells of a local council clerk who went to a diviner's shrine to seek protection from the malice of those from whom he had extorted money, but who neither expressed contrition nor received censure.[5] Generalizations drawn from the particular can be misleading. Such opinions do not seem to distinguish between principle and practice.

'The orthodox ethical norm does not consist in the ordinary behaviour of men.'[6] There may indeed be some element of utilitarianism in an individual's approach to morality, but a balanced assessment of morality in African traditional religion should attempt to put it in the context of their whole system of belief, as expressed not only in the behavioural patterns of selected individuals but set within the whole framework of ways in which Africans express themselves both individually and in their traditional groups.

According to another opinion, sin consists principally in the harm done to the welfare of a group, or group member, so that stealing, witchcraft, murder and adultery are considered serious sins which, in some cases, are thought to be expiated by paying compensation. But this is only one of several aspects of the African view of morality. Crimes such as witchcraft, murder and theft also require ritual purification for their expiation because they are considered offences against God or the deities. Those with hidden sins are believed to be forced to death-bed confessions by their consciences. This is called *Isa n'ọnu*, forced confession.

There is no doubt that traditional African morality emphasizes social rather than individual moral responsibility but the supernatural takes precedence over both social and personal dimensions of morality. This is because, as we saw, the overriding concern in the African system of belief is the maintenance of harmony in the ontological order, in which man himself is a vital force. Certain principles in man link him with the different forces: his *Obi*, Breath, is his life-force and links him with other cosmic forces; his *Chi*, Spirit-guardian, links him with the Creator; his *Eke*, Ancestral soul, links him with the rest of the human community, dead and living, and his *Mmụọ* or Spirit, 'the real person' is the subject of all his activities. The basis of all morality is therefore seen as the maintenance of a harmonious relationship between man and these other groups of beings. One therefore finds that although morality is conceived in the idiom of a relationship with the mystical forces, it has at the same time supernatural, social and personal dimensions. However, one aspect may be emphasized in a particular case, depending on the case in question.

Some offences are primarily seen as offences against God, others are against the deities or ancestors. Still others are deemed to be directed against human society and some compromise the integrity of the individual. However, all offences are disruptions of the harmonious relationship in the ontological order. Indeed, one could say that the gravity of an offence is judged by how far it disturbs the ontological order. The greatest offences are those which threaten the moral order itself, and this is borne out by an examination of the Igbo moral code.

The moral code

The corpus of Igbo law is called *Omenala*; in literal terms, this means the customs of the land; theologically, it means the customs sanctioned by the Earth-deity. *Omenala* embodies the moral code as well as the customs. Igbo terminology and traditions distinguish moral and religious offences from purely social ones. Of course, an offence may be anti-social, immoral and irreligious all at the same time, and many are. The Igbo use the term *Ajo ihe* to denote anything they consider evil. *Ajo ihe* might denote physical *or* moral evil, a misfortune *or* a deliberate misdeed. A moral fault, on the other hand, is called *mmehie*, a transgression; *ajo oru*, bad deeds or *njo*, a sin. Each implies *deliberate* transgression. The term *Nso*, forbidden, is used to describe offences which disrupt relations with the supernatural forces. Each deity and spirit has its set of *Nso* or taboos. The ancestors, too, have their *Nso*. The most serious among the *Nso* are *Nso Ala*, taboos of the Earth deity. These are believed to threaten the stability of society itself as well as that of nature, because the Igbo say that apart from the sky, everything else rests on the earth. The most heinous of the crimes against nature are the *Aru* or abominations. Some abominations are immoral acts, others include the acts of irrational beings; it is *Aru*, for example, for a hen to hatch just one egg.

The Igbo sense of sin is also evident in their judgments on the gravity of certain offences and their sanctions and expiations. Lack of choice or of deliberation are recognized as attenuating factors when estimating the gravity of certain offences, and this clearly bears out the view that traditional morality sometimes has a sense of sin as a deliberate offence of a free will. This principle does not apply to certain categories of sins which threaten the ontological order, or *Nso*. The birth of twins is *nso*. It is *nso* for a child to cut its upper teeth first. Children guilty of these offences are thrown away or given to the Nri priests. It is *nso* if an animal gives birth to one of another species. Abortion is also an *nso*. These are seen as evidence that the natural order has been disturbed and must be redressed.

One may ask: how could a people who hold to such

barbaric customs appreciate morality? Religion sometimes cuts across morality and African religion is no exception. Failure to make this vital distinction has led many authors to absurd conclusions about the moral sense of the African. When Abraham wanted to sacrifice his son Isaac, he knew that murder was immoral, but he believed that he was doing the will of God. The Igbo who throw away their twin babies do so with the religious conviction that it is the precept of *Omenala*, ordered by the Earth Deity. The Igbo also see a logic in these beliefs. *Afube bu Aru*, abnormality is an abomination. Men are usually born one at a time, therefore two babies striving to be born at the same time must be an abnormality, a threat to the natural order, or an indication that ontological harmony has been disrupted. Herbert Marcuse would seem to agree with this logical conclusion when he observes: 'however we may define the word science in some philosophical or epistemological system, it is clear that it begins with the use of previous observation for the prediction of the future'.[7]

An analysis of the Igbo reaction to a number of specified offences serves to illustrate this: murder, theft and adultery are all heinous crimes in the Igbo moral code, but the nature and gravity of each of them changes according to the circumstances, and they have both social and supernatural repercussions.

Murder

Respect for human life ranks high in the Igbo moral code. The taking of human life is universally held as a great evil in Igboland except where such killings are commanded by religion – in the case of twins, for instance. Every illegal taking of human life is called murder, *Ochu* – whether it be voluntary or involuntary. Every *Ochu* is *Aru*, a heinous abomination and an offence against the Earth Deity. Traditional sanctions for murder clearly distinguish between the social, moral and religious aspects of the crime. Unpremeditated murder is *Ochu' Oghom*, accidental murder, the killer is notified and given opportunity to flee the town. He may return after three years when feelings have

calmed down, and is received back on payment of a
specified sum of money in compensation to the relatives of
the deceased.

If the murder is premeditated, the houses and property
of the culprit's family are destroyed. If he has not fled, he is
expected to hang himself. If he flees, he must remain in
exile for seven years, otherwise he can be slain on sight by
the relatives of the murdered man. At the end of the period
of exile, he may return on payment of an agreed compensation to the family of the deceased and the offering of
expiatory sacrifices, *Ikpu Aru*, to Ala, the Earth Deity. These
are necessary to restore the balance and harmony which has
been disturbed by the offence.

Theft

Theft is severely punished. A thief caught in the act may be
summarily killed, or the execution may take place after a
public mockery. The culprit is dragged through the streets,
squares and market places and passers-by may load him
with torments and insults. This treatment continues until
he dies. Notorious robbers may be caught and sold into
slavery, or murdered by a killer hired by the community.

The yam is the staple food of the Igbo and the mainstay
of the economy. Theft of yams, therefore, threatens the
very foundations of society. It is not only *ajọ ihe*, an evil
deed, but *arụ* – an abomination and the penalties are
accordingly heavy. A person convicted of yam theft
becomes an *Osu*, or outcast. This status is passed on indefinitely to all his offspring.

Adultery

Adultery is condemned whether it is committed by a man or
a woman, though the law is more severe on women. This is
probably because prostitution destroys fertility in women
and infertility threatens the existence of the community.
Besides, in a polygamous system, the wives do not have
exclusive rights over the husband. A man convicted of

adultery pays a statutory compensation to the wronged husband. A woman caught red-handed could be beaten up and sent home to her family. She is also bound to confess her hidden sins of adultery, as failure to confess may cause difficulties in childbirth. At Awka, a woman who committed adultery would go to a titled man in her family and, kneeling before *Okpo ozo*, the emblem of titled men, would confess her sins and divulge the names of her partners in adultery. The titled man then calls her husband and pleads with him to let bygones be bygones. A fowl is then killed and eaten by the couple and all the titled men present. Basden reports that infidelities after engagements and before marriage are confessed to the *Umu ada*, female relations of the husband, in a rite called *Isa ifi*, confessing faults. Adultery is therefore a social as well as a moral fault which brings down supernatural sanctions on the offenders.[8]

The foregoing examples clearly illustrate how Igbo morality takes into account attenuating and aggravating circumstances in evaluating the gravity of an offence.

Is morality referred to God?

To whom is morality referred, God or other subordinate beings? This is an even more controversial issue. Monica Wilson has argued that 'since the traditional religions of Africa were not monotheistic, the sources of retribution conceived were diverse. They include the shades,· the heroes, living senior kin and village head men, neighbours and age-mates, all of whom were thought to exercise mystical power'.[9] This statement is basically true as long as it does not exclude God completely from the sphere of morality. *Omenala* are the immediate concern of Ala and *Ndichie*, the ancestors. According to Meek, 'Ala deprives evil men of their lives, and her priests are the guardians of public morality'.[10] Northcote noted that the most heinous crimes among the Igbo are called *Aru*, abomination, or simply *Nso Ala*, taboos of the Earth Deity. Of a person who commits such a crime it is said, *'Omere Nso Ala'* or *'Omeruru Ala'*, 'He defiled the land'.

One God does not *ipso facto* exclude the deities, as the

concept of Western monotheism implies, nor does the interest of the deities in human affairs exclude the intervention of God. This again is an error which results from applying Western preconceptions to African beliefs. Writing about the Igbo, Correia complained, '*Quand un Africain admet que Dieu existe, cela ne le porte pas à se demander ce que Dieu veut*' – 'When an African admits that God exists, this belief does not bring him to wonder what God wants'.[11] But in discussing morality, Parrinder says of West African peoples: 'Though God is generally regarded as upholding the moral laws, and judging men after death in accordance with their actions, many practices seem to have little to do with him'.[12] This statement is more representative of Igbo beliefs and practices than Arinze's opinion: 'Ibo morality is not clearly referred to God. Since Chukwu does harm to no one, fear of the spirits and a narrow utilitarianism elbow him into the background'.[13] Arinze does not seem to distinguish between principle and practice. Moral precepts are one thing and people's behaviour quite another.

Basden also finds a dichotomy in the Igbo approach to morality. According to him, 'Certain delinquencies like murder, theft and adultery, are considered heinous crimes and deemed contrary to the will of God and punishment will surely follow. But actual fear of retribution is not sufficiently strong to check wrong-doing . . . To be found out by his fellow-men is regarded as far more shameful than offending God. In this he is not different from the rest of mankind'.[14]

Thus the rôles of Chukwu and the deities in determining human conduct are not mutually exclusive, they are complementary, not contradictory. This is borne out by the Igbo beliefs about *aru* detailed above. Although Ala, the Earth Deity, has such a determining rôle in morality, the offences specifically referred to her are very limited. *Nsọ Ala*, the taboos of the Earth-Deity cover only a tiny fraction of the spectrum of Igbo moral transgression – *Ajọ ihe* or *Njọ*, evil thing. For example, all forms of theft are *Ajọ ihe*, but only the theft of yams is *Nsọ Ala*. God has assigned the surveillance of the natural order to Ala. This was the explanation which Nweke Ezeamalụ gave me when I asked him why Ala and not Chukwu punishes *Aru*, the heinous crimes which threaten ontological harmony: 'God created Ala and told her if anyone does such and such a thing (e.g. abortion) kill him'.[15]

There is a whole range of other *Ajọ ihe*, evils, which are the joint concern of Chukwu, the deities, and human society. Adultery, for example, is not only an act of injustice against the husband but an offence against God and the deities and may be punished by difficulty – or even death – in child-birth. Hence not only compensation but confession and ritual purification are all necessary to obtain forgiveness.

Nevertheless the Igbo believe whatever the intervening rôle of the deities, the ultimate control of all morality rests with God. Besides the voice of conscience which He put in man, God exercises His control over morality in several ways: first, through His universal providence over the universe; second, through His direct punishment of wrongdoing in this life; third, through the prerogative He has of allotting a good or bad *Chi* during reincarnation cycles, and fourth, through His control of reincarnation itself.

The Igbo believe that order and harmony in the world are under the control of God and are ruled by fixed laws. Good deeds bring order and attract peace, happiness and prosperity. Evil creates disorder and brings suffering, misfortune and death. This principle, already implied in the myths about the origin of evil, was brought home to me by the following story. An elder told me of a time long ago when a series of misfortunes befell his village. Children were dying, women aborting, sickness was rampant, young men would die before they could marry, crop failures were frequent. According to him, *Obodo na agba kpatakpata*, 'The village was burning like a dry bush'. The elders decided to make a pilgrimage to the Arochukwu oracle to discover the reason for these misfortunes. In his oracle, Chukwu said that 'The misfortunes among you are from among you.' He elaborated: 'Your misfortunes are due to the hatred, suspicion, ill-will, sorcery and witchcraft practised by members of the village on their fellow villagers.' As a ritual remedy, the Chukwu oracle prescribed among other things that a shrine to Chukwu be set up in the village itself, and all the male natives with their wives and children should assemble there every eighth day, on Eke market-day to perform rituals. The rituals included making peace among themselves and participating in a communal meal and joyous dancing. My informant concludes that the misfortunes disappeared shortly afterwards.[16]

The lesson of this story is that nature has its own rhythm and logic. Evil begets evil, good begets good. If nature is not cheated irregularities do not occur. The Igbo believe that this is a law of nature which Christianity has not removed. This was the observation of an informant who told me the story of a Christian who, because he was rich, enticed and wedded a girl who was already betrothed to another. The Christian couple has since been without child. The general belief in the village is that their childlessness is due to the offence they committed against the poor man. The couple cannot have children because the offended man has justice on his side, *'Jidere ha ọfọ'*. If, however, they take some kola-nuts and palm wine to him and beg him for forgiveness the obstacle will be removed, otherwise no specialist can help them.

There is a similar belief that all evil-doers, no matter how secret their deeds, are seen by God and never go unpunished. Even if a wrong-doer escapes, his descendants will not. The Igbo sometimes express this conviction in prayers: *'Ihe onye na erorụ mmadụ, ka Chineke na erorụ ya'* 'As a man plans for others, so God plans for him'. If he wishes others good, progress and peace, God will also wish him good, progress and peace. If he plans evil for others, God will also visit him with evil. If an Igbo is cheated, especially by somebody greater and more powerful from whom he has no hope of getting redress, he might console himself by saying: *Ọbụ Chukwu ga ekpe*, 'God will judge', or *'Chukwu omụzikwo anya'*, 'Is God no longer awake?' The most obvious way in which God exercises such judgment in this world is by lightning, as in the saying: *'Onye Emeghi ihe iyi, adagh atụ egbe igwe egwu'*, 'One who does not swear falsely does not fear thunder'. A person killed by lightning is not mourned, for he is deemed to have been punished by God for his sins or those of his relatives.

God's retribution does not end in this world. The Igbo say, *'Ikpe di na ala mmụọ'*, 'Justice is in the spirit-land'. A person who is obviously at fault but blindly and insistently asserts his innocence may also be told, '*Chukwu ga ekpe*', 'God will judge'. '*Chukwu ka ọdi naka*', 'Everything is in the hand of God'. He will judge between us. After death, each person goes before Chukwu to give an account of his life on earth. Those whose conduct in this life is found wanting are punished in several ways. God might punish him by giving him a bad *Chi* who will bring him only bad fortune in his next life cycle. This, it may be recalled, was the fate of Okonkwo, the chief character in Achebe's novel *Things Fall Apart*. Generally, punishment for people who have lived bad lives is exclusion from *Ala-Mmụọ*, the land of ancestors (Igbo heaven) and banishment to *Ama-nri mmụọ na mmadụ*, the intermediate state between the spirit-land and human world (Igbo hell). Such a person cannot reincarnate. But where a person whose life is not exceptionally bad may escape this punishment by performing the necessary funeral rites, God may still inflict a corrective punishment on him by making him reincarnate as an animal or tree: 'Transmigration . . . is regarded as the greatest punishment for the incestuous, the murderer, the witch, and the sorcerer. "*Ilọdigh ụwa na mmadụ*" "May you not reincarnate in human form," is a great curse for the Igbo.'[17]

Notes

1 See chapter 1 pp.12 ff.
2 Idowu, B. *Olodumare* (1962) p.154.
3 Obiefuna, A. 'The Christian Education of Igbo moral conscience', unpublished thesis, Rome (1966) p.28.
4 Correia, I. A. 'Le sens moral chez les Ibos de la Nigéria', *Anthropos*, 18–19 (1923–24) p.880.
5 Field, M. J. *Search for Security* (1960) p.115.
6 Tempels, P. *Bantu Philosophy* (1969) p.118.
7 Marcuse, Herbert *One Dimensional Man* (London, 1972) p.8.
8 Basden, G. T. *Niger Ibos* (1966) p.225. Cf. Jeffreys, M. D. W. 'Confession by Africans', *Eastern Anthropologist* Vol. VI, No.I (Sept. 1952) p.43.

9 Wilson, Monica *Religion and the Transformation of Society*, (1971) p.76.
10 Meek, C. K. *Law and Authority in a Nigerian Tribe* (1937) p.124.
11 Correia, I. A. op. cit. (1923–24) p.880.
12 Parrinder, E. G. *West African Religion* (1968 ed.) p.24.
13 Arinze, F. *Sacrifice in Ibo Religion* (1970) p.25.
14 Basden, G. T. op. cit. (1966) pp.38–39.
15 Tape-recorded interview of Nweke Ezeamalu of Awba, Awka Division.
16 Tape-recorded interview of Amos Chukwukelu, elder of Okija.
17 Uchendu, V. C. *The Igbo of Southeast Nigeria* (1965) p.102.

8 God, life and worship

Having established that there is not only a very clear concept of God but also that God is given a central rôle in the creation and organization of the world, we turn our attention to the presence of God in traditional life and worship, and the rôle of God in the after-life. On both subjects, opinion is divided. By far the majority of writers accept and affirm Westermann's view that Africa's God is a 'withdrawn God' with no temples, priests, nor any form of worship. Others would say that traditional religion is mainly concerned with the worship of the deities, ancestors and mystical forces, but 'God is the last resort when other helpers fail'.[1]

Some writers do not accept these generalizations and have based their theories on reports of varying degrees of worship found in many African societies. Parrinder, in his studies of a select number of West African societies, has classified the degrees of worship into three groups: general worship; partial worship; and belief without worship. Under general worship, he lists the religious practices of the Ashanti, among whom are found not only private shrines, but public temples with priests who give regular worship to God, *Onyame*. He remarks that 'over the whole of tropical Africa the only other people who seem to give similar attention to God are the Kikuyu of Kenya'.[2] Elsewhere he mentions that the Dogon of Mali also have public altars at which regular worship is offered to God. Among the Ewe of Dahomey and Togo, there is only partial worship, since organized worship with temples and priests exists only in certain areas, particularly at Abomey. He lists the Yoruba, Igbo and Bini under the third category, 'belief without worship'.[2]

Although this represents a more scientific and critical approach, its classification seems inadequate for our purpose. The distinction between 'general' and 'partial' is designed to assess the distribution of the public worship of God within a particular ethnic group, and it does not sufficiently bring out the significance of indirect and private worship which may exist where there is no organized public worship. However, this approach does represent a significant departure from the tendency to generalize about the worship of God in traditional religion. Here, I would make a distinction between 'indirect' and 'direct' worship of God, and between 'private' and 'public', since this makes for a better assessment of the varying forms and degrees of worship in different societies. 'Indirect worship' may be defined as worship-responses – the prayers, oblations or sacrifices addressed to God through the intermediary of another spiritual being, be it deity or ancestor. (In 'direct worship', such intermediaries are not needed.) In many African societies, God is believed to be the ultimate recipient of most of the sacrifices offered to the deities, and God is mentioned in many of the sacrifices and prayers offered to the deities and ancestors, sometimes with the expressed wish that they convey these prayers to God. These may also be considered acts of indirect worship. Such is the following prayer, offered by Wammah during a sacrifice to her *Chi*. It was recorded by Reverend John Taylor, a C.M.S. missionary at Abo in 1858:

'I beseech thee my guide (*Chi*), make me good, thou has life, I beseech thee to intercede with God the Spirit (*Chukwu Abiama*) tell him my heart is clean. I beseech thee to deliver me from witchcrafts, let riches come to me, see your sacrificial goal, see your kola nuts, see your rum, and palm wine.'[3]

Some Africans would affirm that *all* worship offered to the deities is indirect because they are his messengers. In this sense indirect worship of God exists in all societies where deity worship exists. However, we are concerned here with how much direct worship of God exists in traditional religion.

Direct worship may be private or public, private being that offered by an individual or a group for their own private ends, public being worship that is offered by society or by a person deputed by society, for the welfare of the group as a whole. Private worship is usually informal and includes every act by which man expresses his submission to the will of God and his dependence on Him, such as prayers, invocations, offerings, sacrifices, expressions of daily speech, naming children. Thus they permeate every aspect of life.

God in traditional life

One is not very long in Igbo country before knowing how much God does exist in the Igbo consciousness and how frequently he features in daily speech. The Igbo do not approach Chukwu only 'in the last resource of extremity, when all other gods, arbitrators, advocates, mediums and mediators have miserably failed', as Arthur Leonard says.[4] This is borne out by W. Romaine, a C.M.S. missionary who wrote in 1869: 'This you always find among the Ibos. They never speak of futurity without admitting *Ahonze Tsukwu*', i.e. 'if it please God'.[5]

According to Talbot, every morning each Ika Ibo raises his hands to heaven, rubs them and says, 'God, I thank you for long life!'[6]

Any unpredictable future is in the hands of Divine Providence. Such cases are primarily the concern of Chineke, not the deities, for only the Omniscient God knows what hope such an uncertain future holds out for man. This was the baffling discovery of Boyle during a conversation with Ekeke, the head priest of Bonny in 1879. He 'called on Ekeke, the head priest of Bonny. . . . After saluting him, as he was building his house, I said, so you are building your house? He replied . . . 'Yes, If God help me, I will carry it through'. I interrogated, 'What? Isineke help you? Not Isiuwu (juju)?' He said, 'No, I mean Isineke (the Almighty)'.[7]

Turning to Igbo daily life, one finds it is equally full of the sense of a divine presence and need of God's care and protection. For morning greetings the Igbo say *Iputago ura*, 'Have you come out well from sleep?' and then go on to enquire about one's family, children and business. If everything is well with the neighbour, the well-wisher says: *Obụ Chukwu*, 'It is God' or 'Thanks be to God'. The congratulatory greeting for a mother who has recently given birth, or anybody who has had a stroke of good fortune is *Chukwu aruka* 'God has done wonders'.

An unexpected child is usually believed to be a special gift from God. After all, man has at his disposal all the traditional medical and spiritual techniques known to the Igbo for procuring children. When these fail, any Igbo knows that his only hope is the mercy and benevolence of God. One Igbo proverb sees God as the only hope of the hopeless: '*Chukwu nwe onye na efu ọhia*', 'God owns the person lost in the forest'. I would mention the case of a colleague of mine, an only son, who was born unexpectedly when his parents – who were not Christians – had lost all hope of ever having a child. In fact, his father had taken a second wife. In gratitude for God's kindness and mercy, and in appreciation of his power and majesty, they named the boy Ifeanyichukwu – 'nothing is impossible to God'. Similar cases are innumerable.

People who have a series of inexplicable misfortunes in spite of conscientious efforts to live good lives and apply the ritual remedies prescribed by tradition and divination, may sometimes lose patience with God and reprimand Him. Such was the cry of a woman after losing her eight children, as reported by Reverend John Taylor: 'Why does God allow others to bear girls and keep them, and see their daughters prosper in the world, and she only suffer from time to time? What bad luck (ajọ chi) has she brought into the world, and what harm had she done to Him?'[8]

This is a very strong argument against the theory of *Deus incertus*. God is very near to the Igbo. He is in continual communication on a person-to-person basis. The Igbo praises, thanks, and sometimes reprimands God if need be. God is a real person to him not a vague power, nor a remote being. Yet, most people who find themselves in an unfortunate situation would not give in to despair but derive comfort from the phrase: *Onweghi ihe gbara Chukwu ghari* 'There is nothing that will surprise God'. Anybody who fears a grave danger would say: *Chukwu Ekwela*, 'May God not

Plate 9 An elder offering morning prayers on the ancestral
shrine. Notice marks of offerings of phallic chalk on the ground

allow this to happen'. The yam is the staple food of the Igbo, and a very successful farmer would take the title of *Eze ji*, or Master of yams. Yet an Igbo saying recognizes that: *Chukwu ji ji jide mma, onye ọwanyere orie*, 'God has both yam and the knife, only those for whom he slices a piece can eat'.

In view of all this evidence to bear out the continuous presence of God in Igbo life and psychology, and their intimate communication with him, it is difficult to justify the assertion by some Igbo writers that 'The Igbo High God is a withdrawn God'.[9] This shows how much past publications prejudice further research.

Prayers to Chukwu

Many prayers are offered to God through the deities, especially *Chi* and *Anyanwụ*. Prayers are addressed directly to God mostly in the form of invocations. These are very frequent:

Thus, when the head of a family wakes up in the morning, he may, after washing his hands, lay a kola or some snuff on the ground, saying 'Obasi-idinenu (Chukwu), watch over me and my children this day'. Anyone setting forth on a journey may ask Chukwu to make the object of the journey successful and bring him home again in safety.[10]

The Igbo morning prayers are addressed to God. Curiously enough, this is the first thing the head of each family does every morning, before he speaks to anyone. A son, or his wife, will bring him a basin of water in front of the Chukwu symbol. The man brings out his *ọfọ* and lays it on the ground, breaks a kola-nut, chews part of it and spits it on his *ọfọ*. He now takes this up and prays to Chukwu, the spirits and his ancestors. Then he confesses his sins (in fact, he confesses his innocence and asks pardon for wrongs he may have committed unknowingly); he asks for blessings for all his well-wishers and curses for those who wish him evil. *Ihe onye na-erorụ mmadụ, ka Chineke na-erorụ ya*, 'As a person plans for others, so God plans for him'.[11]

Here is a model of Igbo morning prayer.

Invocations of God and the deities

Chineke taa Oji	Chineke eat kola.
Chukwu Abiama raa Ochoma	Chukwu Abiama take sweet white chalk.
Obassi di n'elu Ekene	Lord of Heaven, greeting.
Anyanwu na Ezenu Ekene	Son, king of Heaven, greeting.
Ala Nnewi taa oji	Earth-Deity of Nnewi eat kola!
Edo taa oji	Edo eat kola!
Nna Nnaa ha tanu Oji	Ancestors eat kola!
Onye wetara Oji, Wetara ndu,	Who brings kola, brings life!
Ndu k'anyi na ario	We are asking for life!
Ndu nwoke, ndu nyanyi	Life of man, life of woman!
Ogonogo ndu na nka	Long life, and old age.
Gi bu Chineke n'ata n'ogbe	You God, eat whole!
Ma anyi n'ata n'ibe	We eat in pieces!
Chineke bia nara anyi ojia waa	God come break this kola for us,
Makana na anyi enweghi aka	for we have no hands,
Na oku agunyere nwata n'aka	But the fire given to a
adagh arugbu ya	child, does not hurt it.

Confession of sins

Onu kwuru njo gbaghara	Forgive who speaks evil.
Onu kwuru mma gbaghara	Forgive who speaks good.
Mmefie adighi, mgbaghara a ma adi	If there is offence, there would be no forgiveness.
Ma m'egbugh kwo nne nwoke	But I did not kill any man
Nke m'ji megbu nne nwanyi	Nor did I kill any woman.
Ma m'atutughi ihe mmadu	I never removed any man's thing
Nke m'ji eduru nwunye mmadu	Nor abducted another's wife.

Petitions

Ihe anyi na ario bu ndu	We ask for life.
Nye anyi omumu, nye anyi ego	Give us children, give us money.
Nke onye n'eme, ka ona agara ya	Whatever man does let him prosper by it.

Blessings and curses

Ka ndi na-ekwurum mma	Both those who wish me good
Ka ndi na-ekwurum njo	And those who wish me evil.
Ihe onye na eroru mmadu	What one plans for other

Ka Chineke na eroru ya	So God plans for him.
Ọbịara be onye, abiagbu na ya	Let a visitor not maltreat his host
Ọlawa mkpumkpu akwana ya	Nor host poison his guest.
Ọchụ nwa ọkụkọ nwe ada	Who pursues a fowl, will fall.
Egbe bere ugo bere	Let both the kite and the eagle perch;
Nkị si ibe ya ebela, nku kwa ya	whoever tells the other not to, let his wings break.

This is certainly the Igbo worship which the Reverend J. During described in his report of 1878. His rather cynical account shows how distorted his knowledge of this Igbo custom is:

> How they offered their prayers every morning? With their stick toothbrush. When they chewed it to their satisfaction they took it out and slew their hand with it around their head many times and sprinkled spits as they think and said God must eat it, and he must give them cowries (money) and should any of their enemies want them to die, such an one must die. And in front of their houses they planted a tree and pray through it; they said, when they speak to it, the stick conveyed their words to God; all broken plates, cups, placed on the roots of the trees, they said, they gave it to God.(sic)[12]

Altars and priests of Chukwu

According to During's report quoted above, Chukwu's altar at Ossomare was a tree planted in front of the house. Reverend During does not identify the tree, but mentions that broken pots and plates are left at its base. Talbot is more precise, Chukwu's shrine is not a dustbin:

> 'His (Chukwu's) most common symbol is an Ogbu, cotton, or Awha (or Chi) tree, or sapling or a post, some four to six inches high, usually accompanied by round or flat stones, and a pot or pots, containing water and sometimes yellow wood, eggs, phallic chalk cones, round stones and palm wine.'[13]

Talbot confesses, however, that there are places such as Agbaja and Nkanu where no symbols are made. Shelton publishes photographs of altars and shrines dedicated to

Chukwu in the Nsukka division. The individual personal shrines can take several forms: 'cone-shaped earthen altar', 'a live tree called either Ogbu or Alagba', 'a very small house-type structure'. There are village communal shrines called Ọnụ Chukwu, altar of God, or literally, mouth of God. He described one such altar found at Umunne-Gwa village: 'This altar is in the village square, and is set upon a conical earthen mound four feet in height. The altar itself is the wooden carving place atop the earthen mound and its main face is directed towards east, where the sun rises'.[14]

This community altar is very similar to that described by Fr. Arazu as found in Ihembosi.

A public altar which I saw at Aje in Nsukka area was situated at the centre of the market place. It consisted of a round mound made of red clay about one foot six inches in height and two feet six inches in diameter. Behind the mound was a dry branchlet of Ogirisi tree (Newbouldia) about three feet high, cut in such a way that it looked like the head of an animal. The face pointed to the east. Behind this branchlet was a big tree, planted when the shrine was set up.

A private altar which I photographed at Okija in Ihiala division consisted of an earthen mound about six inches high and one foot in diameter with a small earthen bowl sunk into the mound to receive the offerings. An altar for occasional direct sacrifices to Chukwu in some parts of Igboland is much simpler; this is set up when needed and consists of 'a white fowl at the foot of a palm mid-rib'.[15] Meek describes the setting-up: 'He takes a white chicken and hangs it by the feet in a cleft piece of bamboo which is stuck into the ground.'[16] An Ogbu or Chi tree is planted beside the bamboo and an earthenware bowl is buried at the foot of the tree, face upwards to receive the offerings. This sacrifice, called Aja Eze Enu, 'Sacrifice to God, king of the sky', is more widely practised throughout Igboland, as we shall see.

Chukwu has no priests like Ala, Earth Deity, or other nature deities, but as with Chi, the spirit-guardian and Ndichie, the ancestors, the minister at the cult of Chukwu can be any adult, a head of the family, chief of the clan or Ikenye, the oldest man in the village.[17] Sacrifices to Chukwu through Anyanwụ, according to Meek, may be made by anyone. According to Shelton, among the northern Igbo the daily prayers and regular sacrifices are offered to Chukwu by the head of the family at the family shrines and by the *Onyisi* or head man of the clan at the communal altars. One of Arinze's informants mentions that *Aja Eze Enu* is made by a *dibia*, medicine-man. At Ihembosi, sacrifices to Chukwu on the occasion of the annual Chukwu festival are made by the eldest man in the clan and no one else.

Direct public offerings to Chukwu

Our data on this topic suggest that many Igbo groups make sacrifices direct to Chukwu. Such sacrifices are not as rare as is often suggested. We shall try and determine here which and how often direct sacrifices are made to God, and how many types of such sacrifice there are.

Meek says that anyone may sacrifice to Chukwu through Anyanwụ 'when he feels inclined or when directed to do so by a diviner'.[18] Shelton finds that 'in some villages there is regular daily worship of the High God, and in other villages worship tends to occur either on an annual festival day dedicated to the High God or when the individual faces a particular problem which requires his supplication of God rather than one of the Arụsi'.[19] According to Talbot, 'As a rule sacrifices are made to God at the two great festivals of seed-time and harvest'.[20] Annual festivals of Chukwu seem to have been widespread in Igboland in the past. Ihembosi is not therefore an exceptional case, though its rarity nowadays shows that this practice is on the decline and bears out the hypothesis that the introduction of Christianity has contributed to the corruption of African traditional worship of God.

Anozia gives an interesting example from among the Oguta of the Oru clan where sacrifice to Chukwu takes the form of an initiation rite, fitting the initiate to set up a symbol of Chukwu before which he can henceforth offer daily prayers as already described: 'There are two stages to full initiation into the cult of Chukwu. The first stage was

open to men, but only men, with family responsibilities.
The second stage was open to men who had passed what my
informant describes as the age of manhood'.[21] Four types of
direct sacrifices to God can be identified: The rites of *Igba
Mkpu Chukwu*, celebrating God's mound; *Aja Eze Enu*, sacrifice to God, King of Heaven; *Iruma Chukwu*, installing the
altar of God and *Ikpalu Chukwu Ugbo*, making a sacrificial
boat for God on marriage.

Ime Chukwu or Igba Mkpu Chukwu (festival of God)

This rite as celebrated in Ihembosi has already been
described in the Introduction.

The rite which is called *Igba Mkpu Chukwu*, celebrating
Chukwu's shrine, in Ihembosi is called *Ime Chukwu*, God's
festival, at Aje in Nsukka Division. It takes place twice
annually, once before the planting season and again soon
after the first harvest has been gathered in. In preparation
for the festival the shrine, which is situated in the centre of
the market-place, is decorated with fresh palm fronds. This
festival is one of the few religious festivals which is celebrated by the whole village together. As in Ihembosi, the
participants are the elders, but the officiating priest is not
the eldest elder but the *Oga Ahia* or market master. These
are apparently custodians of the Chukwu shrine as well as
market wardens. This arrangement may be purely one of
convenience because the wardens are in a better position to
attend to the individual worshippers who occasionally bring
their offerings and petitions to the shrine. The sacrifice
consists of libations of palm wine and liquefied white chalk
poured on the altar of God, and the immolation of a goat.
The shrine is smeared with the blood of the sacrifice, then
the meat is cooked. Some is offered to God on the shrine
and the remainder is eaten by the participants. While pour-
ing the libation and making an offering of the food, the
officiating priest also offers prayers for the welfare of the
group, for a good harvest and for peace and prosperity
within the community.

I visited the *Onu Chukwu*, God's shrine, at Aje a few weeks
after the festival. There was little trace of the blood that had
been smeared on the shrine but there was a paste of

liquefied white chalk on the surface of the mound and stripes where it had run down the sides.

Aja Eze Enu (sacrifice to God, King of Heaven)

The most common direct sacrifice is called *Aja Eze Enu*, Sacrifice to God, King of Heaven. Variations of this name occur in several places. In the Awka area it is called *Ilu onu Anyanwu*, 'setting up an altar of the Sun'. At Nnewi, it is called *Imanyelu Eze Enu Okuko*, 'tying a fowl for the King of Heaven'. The direct sacrifices to God described by Meek, Talbot and Basden vary only in detail from Arinze's description of *Aja Eze Enu*. According to one of my informants, this sacrifice is usually made during the harvest season and the necessary objects include a white chicken, eggs, yams, an eagle's feather and a long pole, *ofolo ngwo*. The minister, usually a *dibia* or medicine-man, ties the chicken, the yams and the feather to the end of the pole with a white cloth. He then plants the pole in the ground with the live fowl and the objects suspended in the air and offers another chicken and an egg at the foot of the pole while saying the following prayer:

'Eze Enu, receive these our gifts for the preservation of our families, our relatives, our friends. Increase our children and our crops, so that by this time next year we may have something to give thee.'

The people standing around answer *'Ofo-o'* 'Let it be so'.[22] The sacrifices to God which Talbot observed are made at the two great festivals of seed-time and harvest. At Aro, an Igbo village, 'if anyone is told by the doctor to make a sacrifice, he generally offers up a white fowl at the foot of a palm mid-rib'.[23] A white fowl hung on a bamboo pole also features in the sacrifices which Meek says are offered to God through Anyanwu in the Agwu Division.[24]

This again raises the question of the extent to which Chukwu is associated with Anyanwu, the sun, and whether *Aja Eze Enu* is always offered to Chukwu through Anyanwu. Basden suggests that the reason why white objects are used in sacrifices to Chukwu is 'because the sun is white, it is thought that the Great God will only accept a white sacrifice'.[25]

Iruma Chukwu (an initiation rite)

Anozia found a type of direct sacrifice to God among the Oguta Igbo group called *Iruma Chukwu*. This literally means 'implantation of God'. *Iruma Chukwu* is an initiation rite performed in two stages, and the objects used are the same as the ones used for *Aja Eze Enu*. For the first stage of *Iruma Chukwu*, the usual suspension of the offerings on a bamboo pole as in *Aja Eze Enu* is preceded by a ritual in which the initiate prays with water and phallic chalk for the health and prosperity of his family and village. One fowl 'is offered in mid-air to Chukwu', while the other is killed and shared in a communal meal.

The second stage of *Iruma Chukwu* requires the services of the oldest man in the village. The bamboo set up at the first stage of the sacrifice is taken down and replaced by another, this time planted between two planks of *ukwa*, iron wood, each about four feet high. The same kind of offerings, a white fowl, yams, an eagle's feather and so on, are tied to the bamboo pole for Chukwu. Then a castrated goat is offered up, along with a second white fowl. These are later slaughtered and shared in a communal meal. The initiation ceremony ends when 'the initiate is brought to sit in the place where, up till now, the prelate had been sitting. He then prays, as he has been taught, with water, chalk and kola-nut',[26] as each elder does every morning.

It would seem that this form of sacrifice was very common among *Ndi oru*, riverine Igbo. I found an Iru Chukwu altar, now very rare, at Ogwuikpele in the Ogbaru Division. It consists of an Ogilisi tree, and an earthenware bowl of water, sunk into the mud floor in the sitting room. Chief Oduah, who owns it, explained that he set it up as soon as he got married. The rituals which were exactly the same as those of Iruma Chukwu, were followed by a sumptuous feast for his contemporaries. Chief Oduah explained that he still worships at Iru Chukwu every morning with the following prayer:

'Chukwu Abiama	Oh God of the Universe
Bia nalụ m nni	Come and take food
Nalụ m Oji	Take kola-nuts
Nalụ m mmanya	Come and take drinks.'

He then offers the objects to Him and receives an answer. When asked how the answer is received he said: 'Don't you see that this shrine of Chukwu faces upwards? The Chukwu in heaven talks to it, and it talks to us when we are asleep and tells us what is going to happen. This Chukwu below is the *Ukọ* or servant of Chukwu above'.[27]

Ikpalụ Chukwu Ụgbọ (making a sacrificial boat for God)
From the Ogwu Division, Dr. Ezeanya reports yet another form of direct sacrifice to God called *Ikpalụ Chineke Ụgbọ*: making a sacrificial boat for God. The principal objects required for the sacrifice include: a cock, some large yams and a boat-shaped container woven from palm fronds. On the occasion when this sacrifice was observed, it was being offered for the success of an impending marriage by the father of the bride on the advice of a diviner. The officiating priest was the priest of the local Earth Deity, *Ala-Ihe*. Although the sacrifice was offered near the shrine of the Earth Deity, it was not made on the shrine itself. Instead, the offerings were put in the boat and the blood of the cock was sprinkled over it while the priest prayed:

God, who created man, behold this fowl; God, who created man, behold *Ugwuaku* (the prospective bride), my child, protect her for me. Offspring is the main thing in the world. God, who acts according to his designs, give her children. Preserve her husband to be. Give him the means of giving me wealth to eat. If she gives birth to a female child, it will live, if a male, it will live. May she not have difficulties in childbirth. May her health be good, may the health of her husband be good. Prayer obtains among the spirits and among men. God, treat me well: I am asking for goodness. My son-in-law shall give me things and I shall eat. Love will exist between us. God, that is what I ask for, Ihe land! Spirits of Ihe! God the Creator! I thank you. I have finished.[28]

Conclusion

All the evidence discussed above has shown that neither *Deus Absconditus*, the hidden God, or *Deus Otiosus*, the idle God, is a fair description of Africa's God, and that it can be misleading to generalize about the worship of God in Afri-

Plate 10 An elder worshipping before the shrine of Anyanwụ
na Eze enu (God, King of the sky). Notice the Ọfọ (symbol of
ancestral authority) in his right hand

can traditional religion. There are hundreds of tribes in
Africa which, though they have some beliefs in common,
have developed different habits of worship over the years.
One group may emphasize one form of worship-response
more than another. Some have highly developed ancestor
cults, others have elaborate pantheons and very organized
cults of their different deities. Anthropological reports
show that some African communities have developed
organized public worship of the Supreme Being while
others have not. This does not mean that we already know
everything there is to know about the African communities
and their religious beliefs. Generally, our knowledge as it

stands at present allows us to affirm that deism in the sense of belief in God without worship is not a distinguishing characteristic of African traditional religion. The types of worship given to God vary in different African societies. But, by and large, theism is certainly more common in Africa than deism. Every African society has some form of worship of God, be it direct or indirect, public or private.

Belief in many deities and the ancestral cults has obscured and overshadowed the worship of God. Mediation is a common feature of the African way of life. The number and status of the intermediaries enhances the prestige of the One addressed, and though no organized public worship of God exists – other than that made through the intermediary deities – this may surely be described as indirect worship of God. To the African, this does not mean worship of secondary importance. The two explanations given for this are that the Africans think that the exalted position and dignity of God demands that He be approached through intermediaries, and that the African presumably has the pious feeling that he is inadequate and the intermediaries will present his offerings better than he can.

Even in societies where only indirect public worship exists, individuals do approach God directly in their private devotions. Some would say that this happens only in extreme situations or crises, but this is not necessarily so. Writers have reported many Africans' awareness of the presence and rôle of God in their lives. This is shown by the constant mention of the Supreme Being in everyday life, in proverbs, greetings, exclamations, the naming of children, oaths and invocations of His name. These are forms of worship-responses and are included in the definition of worship in its broadest connotation.

Finally, there are many societies, like the Igbo, which have organized public direct worship of God although denied by earlier reports. This suggests the necessity of continuing research even in those communities already extensively studied. It is also true that since the introduction of Christianity and Islam certain forms of worship of the Supreme Being in some communities have ceased. It is reported that in some places, believers in traditional religion have been labelled 'idol worshippers' and they have reacted by confining themselves to the worship of the deities and ancestors, leaving the worship of God to Christians.

A more convincing explanation for the disappearance of many forms of the worship of God was given to me by Chief Oduah. The rites of *Iruma Chukwu* are communal rites involving the participation of his age-group members. Since most of these have either died or become Christians he could no longer perform them. Most of the sacrifices to God described here are peace offerings which end with a communal meal. Where the group sharing this meal has disintegrated, the rites also gradually disappear. The areas where direct sacrifices have survived in Igboland are places which are least affected by Christianity.

One would also accept the suggestion that a vast number of sacrificial offerings in traditional religion are directed towards the restoration of the ontological order. Since God, the Founder of this order, is believed to be above its laws, having handed over its control to the intermediaries, man is more concerned with propitiating these intermediaries whenever the order is thought to have been upset.[29] This seems to be borne out by the fact that the offerings made to the Supreme Being reported in this chapter are peace and thank-offerings made at seed-time, harvest time or at initiations. They are made, as it were, to usher in the next stage of a continuing ontological cycle rather than repair its broken chain.

Notes

1 Smith, E. W. *African Ideas of God* (1961) p.30.
2 Parrinder, B. G. *West African Religion* (1969) pp.15 ff.
3 Crowther, S. and Taylor, J. *The Gospel on the Banks of the Niger* (1968 ed) p.348.
4 Leonard, A. G. *The Lower Niger and its Tribes* (1968) p.424.
5 CA3/034/1-9. Niger Missions, Quarterly Journal Extracts by W. Romaine, Native Pastor (Onitsha, 1859–1872).

6 Talbot, P. A. *Peoples of Southern Nigeria*, Vol. II (1926) p.40.
7 CA3/07/1-6 Niger Missions, Extracts from Annual Reports by James Boyle (Bonny, 1874–79).
8 Crowther, S. and Taylor, J.   op. cit. (1968) p.309.
9 Uchendu, V. C. *The Igbo of Southeast Nigeria* (1965) p.94.
10 Meek, C. K. *Law and Authority in a Nigerian Tribe* (1937) p.25.
11 Arinze, F. A. *Sacrifice in Ibo Religion* (1970) p.25, cf. Anozia, I. P. 'The Religious Import of Igbo Names', unpublished thesis (1968) p.25.
12 CA3/015/1 Niger Missions, Journal Extracts of Rev. J. During (Osomare, 1878).
13 Talbot, P. A. op. cit. (1926) Vol. II, p.41.
14 Shelton, A. 'The presence of the Withdrawn High God in North Ibo Religious Belief and Worship', *Man* (1965) p.15.
15 Talbot, P. A. op. cit. (1926) Vol. II, p.42.
16 Meek, C. K. op. cit. (1937) p.22.
17 Anozia, I. P. op. cit. (1968) p.62.
18 Meek, C. K. op. cit. (1937) p.22.
19 Shelton, A. op. cit. (1965) pp.16 ff.
20 Talbot, P. A. op. cit., II, p.42.
21 Anozia, I. P. op. cit. (1968) p.62.
22 Arinze, F. A. op. cit. (1970) p.54.
23 Talbot, P. A. op. cit., II, p.42.
24 Meek, C. K. op. cit. (1937), p.22.
25 Basden, G. T. *Niger Ibos* (1966) p.61.
26 Anozia, I. P. op. cit. (1968) p.63.
27 A tape-recorded interview with Chief Oduah of Ogwu Ikpele, Ogbaru division, July 1974.
28 Ezeanya, S. in Dickson, Kwesi A. and Ellingworth, P. (eds), *Biblical Revelation and African Beliefs* (1969) p.41.
29 Taylor, J. V. *The Primal Vision* (1969) p.80, quoting Jahn, Janheinz *Muntu*, p.115.

9 God and the after-life

The African traditional beliefs in the survival of the human person after death, in ancestors as the 'living dead' and in reincarnation suggest that there is a strong belief in the after-life. Most writers today admit that all African societies believe in an after-life, but with varying degrees of emphasis. Generally, the after-life is viewed from the point of view of the continuing relationship of the dead with the living and not as the final end of man or of the world. There is very little speculation about 'the last things'. Eschatology either in the sense of the culmination of individual lives, or of human history in general, is of marginal interest in traditional religion. This is understandable, given the African conception of life as a cyclic process of birth, death and rebirth. What is, was, and will be. The centre of concern is the eternal now; since the past and the future are really no different from the present, the fulfilment of man is sought in the present. Consequently, the after-life is conceived in terms of the present life. The environment and social structure of each society are each projected into the invisible world and form the framework of its conceptions of the after-life. In this context, ideas about immortality, judgment and retribution play very little part.

There is not a single reported case of a belief in the end of the world as we know it in the near or distant future. Beliefs about the fate of man in the after-life involving a last judgment and retribution do exist, but they seem to be exceptions rather than the rule. For the most part these exceptions are found in West Africa. The Dogon of Mali believe that after the spirit of the dead has been ushered out of the world of the living with the appropriate funeral rites, it engages in an arduous journey which is a form of retribution for its misdeeds on earth. Even for the good, this lasts for at least three years, after which the spirit is admitted into *Manga*, the Dogon paradise. The Yoruba believe that the ancestral soul, *Iponri*, goes before Olodumare after death for judgment in accordance with the saying 'All that we do on earth, we shall account for kneeling in heaven'.[1] The good go to *Orun Rere*, good heaven, while those who have led wicked lives go to the *Orun Buruku*, bad heaven of broken potsherds which is said to be hot – like pepper.[2] Similarly, Igbo ideas about the after-life involve belief in a kind of judgment and retribution. The good go to *Ala Mmuo*, spirit land, where they continue a life similar to their earthly life and are allowed to reincarnate, while the bad are banished to *Ama nri mmuo na mmadu*, the Igbo hell, and turn into frustrated wandering spirits. Here, in detail, are the Igbo beliefs about the after-life.

Like most other non-literate African societies, Igbo beliefs about the after-life are generally well known to the people but they are not systematically documented and preserved in any one place. One has to extricate them from other beliefs in which they are implied and try to present them as systematically and coherently as possible. Here, Igbo beliefs about the after-life are reconstructed mainly – but not exclusively – from their ideas about death, their funeral rites, their beliefs about life in the spirit-land and reincarnation. Some of the ground already covered, for example, the ancestors, man and morality, includes references to the after-life from which we can also learn. Let us first examine the Igbo concept of death.

Ina Ulo (death is going home)

Death is not the end of life. It is rather the end of one phase of life and the beginning of another. Many Igbo funeral songs describe death as *ila ulo* 'going home' or *ila ala Mmuo* 'going home to the spirit-land'. Taylor wrote down this brief song sung during a funeral procession which he observed at Onitsha in 1857:

Ozu, wunrugo	This is the dead body of him that is dead.
Ola na ulo moa (sic)	And is gone into the world of spirits. (sic)[3]

Another song spells out the doctrine of death in greater detail. This was sung by the Umuada, the daughters of the clan during the wake of an elder who had lived a long and blessed life and ended it in Ọnwụ Chi – God's death.

Nwanne laa na udo	Brother go home in peace
Nwanne laa na udo	Brother go home in peace.
Ọlawala na ebe osiri bia n'uwa	He has gone home from where he came into the world.
Ọnwụ, Ọnwụ, Ọnwụ	Death, Death, Death
Ọlawala n'ebe osiri bia n'uwa	He has gone home from where he came into the world.
Chukwu akporogo ya	God has taken him.[4]

Hence, according to these songs, death is not a disaster, it is rather 'going home'. This is very clearly illustrated by the term the Igbo use on this occasion. Usually, the word for death is Ọnwụ, but it is wrong and is regarded as indecent to say of a man ọnwụọla, 'he is dead', but rather ọla la, 'he has gone home'. Many of the rituals performed at the funeral rites are, as we shall see, symbolic preparations for the deceased to enter the spirit-land. 'When a man dies,' writes Basden, 'he is alluded to as having "gone home" or simply as having gone to the spirit world'.[5]

A natural death, therefore, is not an annihilation; it is conceived as something wholly positive. If, as in the funeral song, death is seen as going home to the place from which man came, Ọlawala n'ebe osiri bia n'uwa, it would appear that the spirit-land is man's real home. Man is essentially a spirit, who comes from the spirit-realm, or pre-natal state, for a brief sojourn in this world – after which he returns. Life goes in a cycle, alternating between the spirit-world and the visible world. Death is the gateway between the two states of existence.

The riddle of life and death and the aim and purpose of man's life on earth are themes of many Igbo songs. One Igbo song compares man's stay on earth to a business trip: the duration is very brief and business-like. Once his time is up, a man must go home whether he likes it or not.

Ahia k'anyi biara n'elu uwa	We are on a market trip on earth,
Azujuru ukpa, azujughi ukpa	whether we fill our baskets or not,
Mgbe oge zuru, anyi alawa	once the time is up, we go home.

Another song compares man's stay in the world to a friendly visit.

Elu ụwa bụ ọriri	The world is a friendly visit
Onyẹ nọcha ya alawa	at the end of which we must go home.

Kinds of death

If death is 'going home', not all who die actually reach home, nor is every type of death a good death. It must be emphasized that the very way a person dies is a clear indication of whether he will reach 'home' or not.

There are three types of death awaiting the Igbo: he may either suffer *Ọnwụ Ekwensu*, violent death (literally devil's death); *Ọnwụ ọjọọ*, bad death, or *Ọnwụ Chi*, natural death. The first two are most undesirable and a man would spend all his material resources in sacrifices, offerings, and making the necessary medicine to prevent the first two.[6]

Ọnwụ Ekwensu (violent death)

This term usually describes the death of any young person especially when due to a violent accident. Of such a person it is said *Ọgbabiri Nwụrụ*, 'he snapped and died'. It is believed that the person has not run the full course of his life nor accomplished the task for which the Creator sent him to the world. He has not achieved his destiny, *akara aka*. He is therefore believed to have been snatched away from life by evil forces. Whatever the actual cause of death, he becomes a purposeless, wandering evil spirit in the spirit-world. He belongs to the class of *Ọgbọnuke*, those contemporaries who died in youth who, disgruntled because they did not complete their term of life nor realize their destiny, try to disrupt the lives of their colleagues still on earth by bringing them misfortunes, sickness or barrenness. The *Ọgbọnuke* are driven away by the rite of *Ichụ aja* or 'driving away evil'. It is strongly believed that all those who suffered violent death must reincarnate to complete their term of life and achieve their destiny.

Comparable to *Ọnwụ Ekwensu* is the death of small children, especially the *Ọgbanje* or 'repeaters'. All dead children become *Ụmụ Ahọ* – evil spirits of children. These spirits are conceived of as mischievous children who try to play annoying tricks on their parents. They bring misfortune on the living and are ritually driven away during the *Igụ Afọ* festival, the Igbo New Year.

Ọnwụ Ọjọọ (bad death)

Some deaths are regarded by the Igbo as bad deaths, *Ọnwụ Ọjọọ*. Bad death is linked with one's conduct in this life, and determines the type of burial one is given and most important of all, it determines a spirit's status in the after life.

'When a man is sick, and it is certain that he must die,' writes Mr. Achu, 'the *Ụmanna* (the members of his patrilineage) have to make sacrifices and pray that he may not die on *Afọ* market-day. If he does this is a bad omen, as it indicates that the man has done something evil, because they believe that a good person does not die on Afo day.'[7] This is *Ọnwụ Ọjọọ*.

Other kinds are suicides, death caused by lightning, leprosy, cholera, smallpox, dropsy. Deaths brought about in such ways are taken to be due to sin. As already stated, it is believed that Chukwu metes out his justice on undetected criminals by striking them dead by thunderbolts through his agent *Amadiọha*, or lightning. Death by dropsy is a punishment for evil-doing, especially sorcery; 'the culprit has escaped human detection, but has not escaped punishment at the hands of the gods'.[8]

Such people are not mourned or buried in their homes but thrown into bad bush, *Ajọ ọhia*. There is no formal announcement of the death and people go about their normal business. The Igbo say, *Ọnọ n'ọruru*, 'he is suffering', because the privilege of *Ikwa Ozu*, full funeral rites, is denied them. Their shadows may not enter the *Okpensi*, Ancestral shrine. Those guilty of very grievous crimes such as suicide, or notorious robbers, witches, sorcerers etc. become *Akalogeli*, wandering evil spirits, at once and are banished to *Ama-nri mmụọ na mmadụ* – the desolate,

unhappy place between the living and the spirit-land. This
is certainly a 'hell to be feared'.

Some who have suffered Ọnwụ Ọjọọ by breaking a minor
taboo, those who die on Afọ day or die of dropsy, for
example, may – after elaborate and expensive purification
rites – receive full funeral rites no sooner than a year after
their death. Then they do become Ndichie (ancestors).

Ọnwụ Chi (natural or good death)

God's death or natural death is a blessing from God. It is the
subject of constant prayer especially at blessings of kola, Igọ
Ọje. Ọnwụ Chi is death that follows a ripe old age. However,
by itself it is not enough to gain a person's entrance to and
ancestral status in the spirit-land. He would also have to
have a surviving son or relative to give him the fitting rites
and feed him, inye ya nni, during the daily ancestral cult at
the Ndichie shrine. Elders who have no surviving male issue
may not get to Ala Mmụọ. A colleague told me how his father
did everything he could to prevent his first son from becoming a Christian, so that he could give him the proper funeral
rites and thereafter feed him daily.

Death rites and funeral rites

A distinction must be made between 'death rites' and 'funeral rites': the purpose of the 'death rite' is simply the
interment of the corpse, whereas the purpose of 'funeral
rites' is to assure the deceased of entrance to the spirit-land.
The Igbo say, ka owere laruo ụlọ, 'so that he may reach home'.
It is therefore a rite of passage.

Although the Igbo funeral song quoted earlier says 'Ozu
anwurugo ọla na ala mmụọ', 'when a man dies he goes to the
spirit-land', it is clear to every Igbo man that entrance to the
spirit-land is impossible without the funeral rites befitting
one's status in life. A simple interment is not enough and
those who have no grown-up children are deeply worried
because their entrance to the spirit-land is not assured. Igbo

funeral rites can best be appreciated if they are viewed as symbolic acts of leading a person home. A person who has not had the benefit of funeral rites has not reached home, *Ǫlarubeghi ụlǫ*. Such a person becomes a wandering ghost and an evil spirit and the peace, status and honour due to the ancestors are lost to it forever. This, for the Igbo, represents a state of punishment in the after-life.

According to Bishop Shanahan:

'The spirit of the dead was restless and confused in the next world if it did not get the type of burial it demanded . . . the pagans were naturally horrified . . . and shook their heads in anger and amazement at the thought of the poor spirit wandering aimlessly. "Poor soul", they said, "poor soul . . . he will be lonely and friendless forever".'[9]

Hence it is regarded as a dreadful misfortune to die and be buried away from home. Such a death is called *Ǫnwụ Nnwufu*, the death of a lost soul. All this explains the seemingly unnecessary expense and inconvenience undertaken to bring home the corpse of a relative who dies hundreds of miles away. Those who work in distant places form tribal unions which guarantee members prompt transportation of their corpse home for funeral in case of death. Burying a person in his home symbolizes union with his ancestors.

Before the funeral, the body of the deceased is symbolically prepared for its journey to the spirit-land by undergoing a ritual washing or ablution with water and an anointing with camwood dye *Ufie*. A ram is killed and its blood allowed to drop into the eyes to enable them to see clearly during the journey. A goat and a fowl are killed and the corpse is smeared with their blood and stuck all over with feathers. By now the corpse looks frightening and like a spirit ready to join the company of other spirits in the spirit-land.

Thus ready for his journey, the corpse is further equipped with whatever is needed to continue life in the spirit-world. He is given his working tools, his gun, bag, some cloth and, if he is a rich man, coins and slaves to attend him. The number of slaves depends on the status of the master. 'They think that a man ought to keep slaves and servants in the next world.'[10]

Then follow a series of rituals, the aim of which is, first, to absolve the deceased of his transgressions and to rid him of all obstacles which could impede his entrance into the spirit-land, then to pray to God that the deceased may reincarnate and bring even greater blessings to the family. Absolution-ary rites are absolutely necessary for titled men. Curiously enough, the Igbo believe that nobody should go to the spirit-land with his titles. At death, rituals almost as elabor-ate as those for taking titles are undergone to rid one's spirit self of these titles. The reason for this is obscure, but the explanation often given is that in the invisible world only one king is recognized – God Himself. 'They do believe that if any person is buried with his titles, he will go to challenge the kingship of God'.[11]

The ritual of absolution is performed when the body has been laid in the grave, before filling it up with earth. In the case of a man it is performed by an old man, whilst in the case of a woman by two small girls, who must be virgins. With arms outstretched over the grave they name all the physical deformities and bad habits the deceased had when alive, and ask the deceased not to return with these in his reincarnation. The grave is then filled up and some yams are left on it. These are supposed to be the yams he will plant in the spirit-world. Yam-growing is the principal occupation of the Igbo.

In several areas, such as Achi in the Ogwu Division and parts of the Aguata Division, the funeral rituals are brought to a close with the *Aja Eze Enu*, 'sacrifice to the King of the Sky'. This is the sacrifice offered directly to God and the end of the funeral rites is one of the rare occasions when it is made. I have no reason at all to doubt Mr. Achu's explana-tion of the significance of the rite: 'The sacrifice is offered on this occasion to ask God to receive the dead and to keep him in peace'.[12]

Life, death and reincarnation are directly and completely under the control of God. It is generally taken for granted, argues Basden, that 'when men have run their course on earth, they return to their Master, the Supreme Being, and live with him in the spirit-world'.[13] But the goal of life after death is not fully achieved by *ilaru ulo*, 'going home to the Creator'. One has to reincarnate and reincarnation is com-

pletely controlled by Chukwu. The anxiety of the Igbo over
their lot in the after-life is further heightened by the fact
that reincarnation is more or less subject to the good
behaviour of the spirits in the *ala mmụọ* or spirit-land.
According to Basden: 'Should they be so unfortunate as to
arouse the *ira* of their master, (God) they are in danger of
being banished to *ama-nri maw na madụ*, an intermediate
state between this material world and the spirit world'.[14]
Thus retribution in the after-life has its place in their cyclic
conception of existence. 'Going home' to the spirit-land is
not a terminal stage, as the more fortunate among those
reaching home would be allowed by the Creator to reincarnate. The eventful world of the living with its bright sun-
light and its fascinating traditional life is preferable to the
gloom and monotony of the spirit-land. Evil conduct in this
life may be punished by either exclusion from the spirit-
land, banishment to *Ama-nri mmụọ na mmadụ*, being forbidden to reincarnate, or being given a bad *chi* during the next
term of life on earth. This last option would bring a series of
misfortunes and could eventually end with the victim's
exclusion from the spirit-land and from the life-cycle. This
is probably what Basden means in the passage quoted
above. The Igbo think of the after-life as essentially
dynamic.

Funeral rites for Ọnwụ Ọjọọ (bad death)

The funeral rites for victims of *ọnwụ ọjọọ* differ in many
ways from those of *ọnwụ chi*. The distinction made between
the one and the other bears out the fact that one's status in
the after-life is dependent on moral conduct; bad death is
thought to be punishment for bad conduct. This becomes
evident when one examines funeral rites for victims of bad
death in detail, for the normal funeral rites are preceded by
lengthy and elaborate rites of absolution and purification in
the case of 'bad death'.

   Not all victims of bad death are given the final funeral
rites; sorcerers, witches, notorious criminals, those killed by
lightning and so on are not given any funeral rites at all.
Their evil lives are thought to provide enough evidence for
them not to be admitted to the spirit-land. Funeral rites and

purificatory sacrifices are of no avail for them. They are damned and will forever remain wandering evil spirits. The Igbo believe that sometimes the Earth deity inflicts such people with a long and torturous illness which eventually forces them to confess their crimes, *isa n'onu*, before their death.

Final funeral rites, however, are of great value for some kinds of bad death, especially those which result from the involuntary breaking of taboos – those who die on an *Afo* – and victims of dropsy, smallpox, death in childbirth and so forth.

Absolutions and purifications feature very prominently in these funeral rites, which may not begin until a full year after the victim's death. Meanwhile, their bodies are hurriedly interred in the *Agu* or wilderness, away from their homes, and their death is not announced. The relatives use the interval before the funeral rites to assemble the necessary things for the elaborate sacrifices of purification.

Since these forms of death are usually believed to result from offences committed against one deity or another, the purification rites depict reconciliation with the deity concerned. Those who die on *Afo* day, for example, are believed to have offended the deities of the four days of the Igbo week. The sacrifice of *Aja oriko*, common meal, symbolizes self-purification and the appeasement of these deities. A fowl is killed and roasted and shared by two men and two women who represent the four days of the week. The idea of *n'riko*, communion, is perfectly realized because none of the four participants may put the meat into his own mouth, rather, the two men feed the two women and the women feed the men. This done, other ceremonies follow as described above for *onwu chi*.

Other kinds of *onwu ojoo* such as suicides, leprosy and cholera, are believed to be punishment for grave sins. The purification sacrifices which follow are offered to *Ala*, the Earth Deity.

The sacrifice of *Aja Ikpu Aru*, cleansing the earth, requires the services of a special priest from the Nri or Oreri. The cleansing is done with a sheep, a she-goat and two fowls, *Aghirigha na Abuke* (these are a special species of fowl). The priest takes the livestock in and around the dead man's house and kills them. It is believed that due to his sins, the deceased has not been permitted by the Earth Mother to join his ancestors in the spirit-land all this time. The purification annuls all the taboos or sins holding him back.[15]

Once the cleansing is done, the person is symbolically 'brought home' by the rites of *Nkulata n'ohia*, 'calling back home from the bush'. Some of his relations enter the bush carrying palm leaves, and walk from place to place, beating the trees and grass with these palm leaves calling out the person's name and asking him to return. They continue this until they reach his home where a fowl is killed to celebrate his homecoming. After this, a palm frond the same height as the person is laid on a new mat to symbolize his corpse, and the normal funeral rites may now begin.

The following conclusions may be drawn: there is a firm belief in a life after death. Passage from this life to the next is conceived of as going home to join one's ancestors who form the core of the kinship group of which the kinship group of the living is only a part. One is therefore thought to have reached home when he successfully rejoins his family after death, and is believed to be lost if he cannot join them. Reaching home does not follow automatically after death; it depends on the type of death one suffers and whether one receives the appropriate funeral rites. Funeral rites and ancestral rites are responsibilities within the control of the living relatives, whereas the type of death one suffers – and in some cases the failure to have surviving relatives – are beyond one's control. The Igbo rationalize that these two vital events are under the control of Chi, the destiny or spirit-guardian and the agent of Chukwu, since the fate of the departed so hinges on these two events. The Igbo conclude that a good or bad death, and the fortune or misfortune of receiving or not receiving ancestral rites are in fact retributions for conduct during one's lifetime (sanctions can be carried over to another round of life after reincarnation). Such retributions are immediately attributed to Chi and ultimately to God. The same is true of reincarnation as I shall demonstrate. The *Chi* concept is fundamental to Igbo ideas of retribution in the after-life.

Man in Ala Mmụọ (the spirit-land)

Death is not man's final end. All who die continue to live somehow after their death, whichever deaths they suffered. Even those who received no funeral rites continue to live, but their places of abode and their statuses differ.

The abode of the spirits of the dead, *Ala Mmụọ*, is a carbon copy of the abode of the living. The two differ only in that one is visible and the other invisible. A geographical map of the land of the living would represent the spirit-land in every particular: every town, village and homestead would be situated exactly where it is in the land of the living. However, the land of the spirit is imagined to be underneath the land of the living, probably because the bodies of the dead are buried in the ground. Arthur Leonard succinctly described this: 'In spirit-land every country or locality is marked out or defined just as it is in this world, so that each town, community, or household has its own allotted portion, to which as people die they go'.[16]

The layout of a village in the spirit-land is patterned on the normal Igbo village: there is the *Obi Unọ* or *Ọkpunọ*, residential area; there is the *Agụ*, reserved farmland, and immediately on the outskirts of the village is the *Ajọ Ọhia*, bad bush, where rubbish and all decaying matter is dumped. The bodies of the dead whose lives or deaths are utterly repugnant to the accepted religious standards are also unceremoniously dumped in the *Ajọ Ọhia* to symbolize total rejection and excommunication by both the living and the dead. All these are believed to exist in the *Ala Mmụọ*. The *Ndichie* are believed to reside in an *Obi Unọ* and go out to do farmwork in their own *Agụ*, or farmland. The *Ama-nri mmụọ na mmadụ*, the intermediate place between the living and the spirits where the *Akalogeli*, or restless spirits of the damned are restricted, presumably corresponds to the *Ajọ Ọhia*, or bad bush of the village of the living. Sacrificial victims of the *Ichu Aja*, sacrifices to evil spirits, are usually deposited at road junctions at the outskirts of the town to prevent the *Akalogeli* from entering the village. The idea behind this is that at the road junction, the evil spirits will stop to eat their sacrificial food and then go back to the *Ajọ Ọhia*, or wander off along a route away from the village.

Wandering aimlessly is part of their punishment.

In the same way, the social life of the spirit-land is patterned on Igbo social life. The *Ndichie*, ancestors, enjoy the social life of a normal Igbo village. They have their homes, their wives, livestock, farms and their slaves. This is the reason why the dead are buried with their domestic and professional equipment. In the olden days a man was even buried with his youngest wife and his strongest slaves, but their stay in the spirit-land is believed to be temporary, lasting only until they reincarnate.

This belief not only puts a limit on the amount of property he may take to the spirit-land but also explains why the *Ndichie* are venerated and literally fed for only one or two generations after their death. They are believed to have reincarnated by the end of this time. An informant told me that prayers at funeral rites do not request increased happiness for the deceased in the spirit-land, but for his safe arrival there and his quick reincarnation with even greater prosperity and success. For the *Akalogeli*, there is very little joy and no hope. Their confusion, frustration and isolation are symbolized by the gloom, stench, disorder and darkness of the bad bush where they are dumped.

The social organization of the spirit-land is also patterned on the Igbo. The population is organized in lineages, clans and families and the community retains its class structure with chiefs, elders, lineage clan heads, rich and poor. Life is led as in this world. Women assume their rôle in the home and society and each person occupies the same status and pursues the same profession as during his earthly life. The rich stay rich, the poor remain poor; farmers, traders, wine-tappers, smiths continue their trade, hence professionals are buried with their tools. This is clearly illustrated by an incident reported in the life of the great Christian missionary Bishop Shanahan. In a conversation, he tried to convince a chief of the joys of heaven which could be achieved in the next life by those who became Christians in this life. The chief listened attentively and then asked: 'That is Heaven you say, but tell me, will all the other chiefs be there too? Or . . .'

When he was told that they would not if they continued

in this life as pagans, he answered: 'You see . . . If I go to Heaven and they all go off somewhere else . . . I'd be up there in Heaven all by myself . . . while all my brother chiefs would be down in the other place you speak of . . . No! I'd rather be with my own'.[17]

The Igbo conceive of *Ala Mmụọ* in materialistic terms. Their heaven is a clan heaven. Fulfilment in the next life is achieved when one reaches home to occupy one's proper place among one's own in the next life. Damnation is viewed as an excommunication and a perpetual exclusion from clan life and from the cycle of life and reincarnation. This is not necessarily a defect or an imperfection, nor should it be interpreted to mean that the Igbo concept of life after death is at a rudimentary or primitive stage in an evolutionary process. The full significance of the Igbo conception of the after-life cannot be appreciated if we simply compare it with Christian beliefs. A more critical evaluation would view the problem in broader perspective of the limitation universally found in all human attempts to conceive of the invisible in terms of the visible, the unknown in terms of the known.

Both Christianity and Igbo traditional religion seek answers to the basic questions concerning man's destiny and their answers are basically the same, namely: man's life continues beyond the grave, both the good and the bad continue to live in the next life; there is retribution in the next life based on one's conduct in this life; purificatory rites obtain forgiveness of sins and remission of punishment in the next life. However, there are also important and essential differences. The idea of a place of eternal reward or eternal punishment which is central to the Christian concept of the after-life is completely absent from the Igbo beliefs. Igbo beliefs view life as a continuing cyclic process. After a brief stay in the spirit-land one is allowed by God to reincarnate to continue the joyous cycle of life. The wicked are deprived of the joy of reincarnating.

God and man in the after-life

Chukwu plays a very important rôle in that after-life of every human being, just as he is involved in the process by which man comes into being and the various vicissitudes he passes through during his earthly sojourn. Most of what has already been said can be summarized with special emphasis on the rôle Chukwu plays.

Death alone is not sufficient to make a person a *Ndichie*. Much depends on how a person lived and how he died. Good moral conduct, ripe old age, an *ọnwụ chi* and full funeral rites are all essential requirements before canonization to the ranks of *Ndichie* – the ancestors in the after-life. Chukwu maintains a firm hold on the elevation of any person to the rank of *Ndichie* through his control over the allotment of *Chi* or fate. It all depends on the type of *Chi* one receives from God before he comes into the world. *Ọnwụ Ekwensu*, premature death, *ọnwụ ọjọọ*, bad death and *ọnwụ chi*, God's death, are but results of the contents of the *Chi* received from God before each earthly life. Barrenness and poverty, both of which threaten one's chances of getting befitting funeral rites, are also *Ọnatalụ chi*, fruits of *Chi*.

This raises the thorny question of predestination in Igbo traditional religion. If a person's fate in the after-life depends on what God has predetermined, symbolized by the choice of *Chi* how can one talk of a just retribution in the after-life? Those who end up as *Akalogeli* could well escape blame by claiming that it is their God-given lot. Similarly, those who become *Ndichie* should take no real credit for it because their lot was predestined and not due to their own merit.

The subtle way in which the Igbo explain this paradox of predestination shows that they are not only aware of the problem but have also found a coherent and satisfactory answer – in the context of their system. They explain, for example, that a person who fails to become an *Ndichie* must not blame God; although God prepared the parcels of fortune, his personal *Chi* or spirit-guardian had a chance to choose. If he made an unfavourable choice, his *Chi* is to blame and not Chukwu. A man may ask why God gave him a *Chi* who made the wrong choice and ruined him forever. The Igbo would reply that *Ihe adighi eme jadaa etu ahu*, 'Nothing happens without reason'. If a person suffers such a misfortune it must be the result of his bad behaviour in the previous life for which he has now received retribution. Thus the Igbo phrase *Chukwu ga ekpe*, 'God will judge', means much more to the Igbo than anybody with a Christian or western European background could ever imagine. To the Igbo, it means that God will judge and suitably reward or punish every deed, not only in this world or the after-life, but also in one's subsequent terms of life after reincarnation. God may even extend such a punishment to one's family.

Moreover, His influence over a man's after-life is not limited to control over his Chi. There is a general belief that 'When men have run their course on earth, they return to their master the Supreme Being, *Chukwu*, and live with him in the spirit world.'[18] Details as to how and when the dead reach the Creator vary from one locality to another and are not generally very clear, but it is commonly believed that when a person dies, his spirit remains in this world for some time, wandering restlessly in the vicinity of his home and the other places he used to frequent during his lifetime. After the completion of the funeral rites, the spirit enters the *Ndichie* shrine. Meanwhile his Chi goes before Chukwu for an interview, which has some aspects of a judgment. This is borne out by numerous Igbo sayings which imply that God will judge each individual after death and mete out punishment or reward. For example, a person who is wronged but cannot get redress, may say: *Iga ahu, Chukwu mu anya*, 'You will see, God is not asleep'. Other phrases, like *Chukwu ga ekpe*, 'God will judge', *Ikpe di na be mmuo*, 'Justice is in the spirit-land', certainly refer to this intervention by Chukwu to demand an account of one's term of life in this world. God then decides whether one reincarnates at once or remains for some time in the spirit-land.

About this interview between the departed spirit and the Creator, Leonard writes: 'When the burial rites are concluded, the soul then goes in the presence of the Creator, and after it has been consulted or interviewed by Him, it is permitted according to the wishes it expresses, either to remain forever in the land of the spirits or to return once more to the world.'[19]

After this interview, the spirit settles in the spirit-land as a full fledged *Ndichie*. On earth, this is symbolically celebrated after the funeral rites by the installation of the *Ndichie* shrine inside the *Obi*, reception hall. The new *Ndichie* may now be venerated inside his house. Before the ceremony, 'no food can be offered to the homeless spirit inside the hut, *Obi* or compound'.

Finally, belief in reincarnation illustrates the relationship between Chukwu and the *Ndichie*. The *Ndichie* may reincarnate, but the right to decide to do so is not theirs. 'This rests with and depends entirely on the Creator.'[20]

The above analysis suggests that to ask the question: 'What are the African ideas about the after-life?' may be asking the wrong question. The terms 'this life', 'next life', 'after-life', 'eternal life' are terms borrowed from Euro-Christian philosophy which are foreign to the African system of thought. Life is one continuous stretch of existence and is not split up into 'this life' and 'the next life'. The concept of time is cyclic, not lineal. What happens after death is not the terminal, definitive stage of man's life, it is only a phase in the continuing round of human existence. There is no idea of 'heaven' or 'hell' as a place of reward or punishment – the spirit-land is not a place of eternal repose and happiness, it is rather a transit camp for those awaiting reincarnation to continue the life cycle. The African wants to live and continue to live with a strengthened life-force with each cycle of life. The living are happy that they are alive. The visible world is preferable to the spirit-land, even though the ancestors who live there are believed to be more powerful. Their enhanced powers are used to obtain better living conditions for their living kinsmen in anticipation of when they themselves will reincarnate to enjoy the prosperity thus given to their families. In this sense, African traditional religion is said to be life-affirming in contrast to Asian religions (Hinduism, Buddhism, Islam) and Christianity, all of which can be said to be life-denying. Hinduism, like traditional African religion, has a cyclic conception of life, but whereas salvation for the Hindu consists in liberation from the recurring cycle of birth, death and rebirth, salvation for the African consists in achieving an uninterrupted cycle of life through reincarnation.

African ideas of retribution are worked out in the context of this cyclic conception. Retribution for human conduct is not limited to life after death, but is spread throughout the life cycle and carried over to successive cycles. The greatest evil is to be thrown out of the life cycle through denial of reincarnation. Whether a person may reincarnate or not depends entirely on the Creator. It is not known how God determines this, but it is believed to be linked with one's conduct during earthly life.

The Igbo ideas of retribution are closely tied up with their beliefs about Chi (the spirit destiny). After death, the Chi reports back to God on one's conduct during life. A good life, usually thought of as a resourceful life, is generally rewarded with immediate reincarnation, inasmuch as the living would want this – and divination would confirm it at the earliest opportunity. A bad life, especially an unsuccessful one, may be punished with denial of reincarnation or reincarnation with a bad Chi. A bad Chi will bring its owner great misfortunes in the next term of earthly life. A 'bad death' is due to a 'bad Chi' received as punishment for bad conduct in one's previous life and is a clear sign to the living that the victim has been thrown out of the cycle of life.

Notes

1 Griaule, Marcel *Conversations with Ogotemmeli* (1965) p.189.
2 Bascom, W. *Ifa Divination: Communication between Gods and Men in West Africa* (1969) p.189.
3 Crowther, S. and Taylor, J. *The Bible on the Banks of the Niger, Niger Expedition 1857–59* (London 1968) p.251.
4 I tape-recorded this song at an *Ụmụada* wake-keeping at Nnewi.
5 Basden, G. T. *Niger Ibos* (1966) p.155.
6 Devil (Ekwensu) here must be understood in the sense

of the spirit which excites to violence, as explained in chapter 4.

7 Achu, A. T. 'Life after death in Igbo Religion' unpublished dissertation, Project T.I.M.E. (Lagos 1975) p.11.
8 Basden, G. T. op. cit. (1966) p.278.
9 Jordan, J. P. *Bishop Shanahan of Southern Nigeria* (1971) p.126.
10 CA3/030/1–11 Niger Mission, Reports by Rev. Solomon Perry (Onitsha) 1872–1880.
11 Achu, A. T. op. cit. (1975) p.12.
12 Achu, A. T. ibid., p.14.
13 Basden, G. T. op. cit. (1966) p.283.
14 Basden, G. T. ibid., p. 286.
15 Leonard, A. G. *Lower Niger and its Tribes* (1968) p.186.
16 Leonard, A. G. ibid., p.141.
17 Jordan, J. P. op. cit. (1971) p.30.
18 Basden, G. T. op. cit. (1966) p.283.
19 Leonard, A. G. op. cit. (1968) p.141.
20 Leonard, A. G. ibid., p.150.

Appendix I Is the Igbo concept of God of missionary origin?

After expounding this rather high concept of God, one is tempted to ask whether it is, in fact, native to Igbo traditional religion. Is it not perhaps due to contact with missionaries? Could this belief be traced perhaps to Christian, Moslem or even Jewish influences?

The evolutionary doctrine has been applied to a wide variety of issues including religion. The opinion which denies *a priori* that the concept of God could be found among African peoples is prejudiced by the logic of evolutionism. The general run of the argument is succinctly expressed by this reaction of Emil Ludwig to the prospects of Christian missionary endeavours in Africa. 'How can the untutored African conceive God, ... Deity is a philosophical concept which savages are incapable of framing.'[1] Secondly, it is argued that since the great world religions, Christianity, Islam, Buddism and Judaism, are characterized by monotheism, traditional religion should not lay claim to such a high form of belief. The presumption is that the development of religious beliefs should be proportionate to the degree of the people's social, political, economic and technological development. When a supposed high form of belief is found, every effort is made to show that it is of exotic origin. It cannot be but 'a European conception thinly disguised'.[2] The propounders of this theory forget that there are factors other than evolution which also determine the development of a people's ideas and institutions. Some people may be highly developed in some areas of existence and backward in others.

Very few writers today would question the existence of the concept of God in African traditional religion, but some may still argue that it is due to Christian or Moslem contacts.

Despite the abundant evidence that exists in myths, names and proverbs (see the first three chapters), Fr. Alves Correia, a Portuguese missionary, suggested about half a century ago that the concept of God among the Igbo, like the names by which He is now known, were introduced by missionaries. He observed that in the process of composing an Igbo catechism, Fr. Volger rejected the names *Osebuluwa* and *Chukwu*, suggested by some catechists. The former was discarded as very doubtful because the image of a 'god' called *Ose* was found represented as carrying the world. The name *Chukwu* was very uncertain because the oracle of the Aro people was called by the same name. His suspicion of missionary influence was all the more strengthened, as he said, by the fact that: 'Each time I went to ask a pagan fresh from the bush about whom 'Cuku' or Chineke was, I was greeted by a snappy – 'Amam', 'I do not know'. On the other hand, the pagans who have become familiar with the whites feel offended at the suggestion that they do not have a belief in God (although they do not bother to express their belief in any way).'[3]

The name *Chineke*, now very widely used among southern Igbo groups, he argues, owes its diffusion – as we have said – to its use in the Anglican Igbo translation of the Bible. Correia's doubts and suspicions do not seem to rest on very strong grounds. Questioning people on the streets of an urban area is not the best way to research into the people's traditional beliefs. Perhaps Correia did not know enough Igbo to know that *Amam* in the context he described means 'Mind your own business' and not 'I do not know', as he supposed. However, Correia is not the only writer to express this misgiving. Green says that she is not so sure that there exists the concept of a Supreme Being among the Agbaja Igbo. She writes:

'As for ci, the spirit who creates people and whose name as in Chineke has been taken by the Christians to denote the creator, it is difficult to know what the real Ibo significance of the word is. 'Ci' and 'Eke' together create an individual, but each person is thought of as having his own 'Ci' and whether, over and above this there is any conception of a universal 'Ci' seems doubtful!'[4]

Other writers, while admitting that the concept of God

does exist in Igbo traditional religion, have produced arguments to show that one or other of his personal names was coined by the missionaries. Dr. Ezekwugo in his yet unpublished thesis argues that the traditional personal name for God in Igbo is *Chi*. He traces the history of how the missionaries adopted the names *Chukwu* and *Chineke* as the personal names for God, and observed that there is an evolution in the writings of early Protestant missionaries whereby the name *Chukwu* was gradually abandoned in favour of *Chineke*. This, he explained, was due to the discovery of the fact that *Chukwu* was in fact the great Arochukwu oracle and not the High God. Thus, Bishop Crowther in his first book, *Iso Ama Ibo Primer*, published in 1857, employed the name *Tsuku* for God, but in his next work *Vocabulary of the Ibo language*, published in 1882, he noted that there are three major dialects. In Isuama Igbo, God is *Tsuku*, the Great God. In Bonny (Owerri Igbo), it is *Tsineke*, God the Creator. It was in this book that he used a new word, *Chi*, for the first time.[5] By the turn of the century when the work of translating the Bible was begun (1905–1912), *Tsuku* was already obsolete. *Chineke* alone was used throughout. But *Chineke*, continues Ezekwugo, never existed as a word before the arrival of the missionaries. Rather *Chi* and *Eke* are two *different* words for two *different* creative principles. Jointly, they are responsible for the creation of each individual. Dr. Ezeanya explains that the word *Chineke* must have originated thus: 'The early missionaries asked the natives: "Who created you?" and receiving the answer *"Chi-na-eke"*, understood it to mean "Chi the creator" or "Chi who creates".'[6]

This hypothesis is based on a number of assumptions. It is assumed that the name Chineke did not exist before the arrival of the missionaries. No proof was given. On the contrary, the missionary writings to which the author referred knew the two names of God and the dialectal areas where each was in use. This shows that both must have been in use before the missionaries arrived. It was further assumed that the missionaries coined the name *Chineke*, and also assumed is the way they coined it. The arguments do not sound convincing. *Chi* and *Eke* are indeed two creative principles but both are creatures of God. God is the Creator of everything. The rôles Chi and Eke play in the creation of man are minimal, and in any case, it is Igbo belief that these rôles are assigned to them by God. It is therefore most unlikely that an Igbo would reply to the question, 'Who made you?', 'Chi and Eke'. After all, *Chukwukere*, 'God-created', is a popular Igbo name.

Christian missionaries opened their first stations in Igbo country in 1857. I have studied most of the reports and correspondence of these first missionaries in the Church Missionary Society archives in London. They all confirm the existence of the concept of God in the Igbo traditional religion. Each of the names analysed above, *Chukwu*, *Chi* and even *Chineke*, was used by the Igbo of that period to designate God. Many examples can be quoted from the records of Reverend J. Taylor, the first Christian missionary to settle in Igboland.[7] We have both documentary evidence and an oral tradition which prove beyond doubt that the concept of God and his personal name of *Chukwu* were both known long before the arrival of the missionaries.

As early as 1789, about a century before the first missionary arrived in Igboland, Olaudah Equiano, an Igbo slave-boy sold to the West Indies, affirmed a concept of God when he wrote:

As to religion, the natives believe that there is one creator of all things and that he lives in the sun and is girded around with a belt that he may never eat or drink; but according to some, he smokes a pipe which is our favourite luxury. They believe he governs events, especially our deaths or captivity . . . [8]

It is not true that the missionaries mistakenly appropriated the name of the Arochukwu oracle for the Igbo High God. In fact, long before the missionaries began their work in Igboland, the first explorers, among whom incidentally was Crowther himself, clearly distinguished between *Chukwu*, the oracle of the Aros, and *Chukwu*, the Igbo High God, but noted the identity of their names:

The Igbos all believe in an Almighty-being, omnipresent and omnipotent, whom they call Tshuku, whom they constantly worship, and whom they believe to communicate directly with them through his sacred shrine at Aro. But they speak also of another and a distinct Deity, who at Abo is known as Orissa, but throughout other parts of Igbo, as Tshuku – Okike 'God the creator, or the Supreme God'.[9]

Therefore, the name *Chukwu* was being used to designate the Supreme Being before the arrival of the missionaries and not introduced by them. On the contrary, our data seem to suggest that the crafty Aro sacrilegiously renamed their oracle *Chukwu* to enhance its prestige among the other Igbo groups. It had previously been known as *Ibinọkpabi*. The Aro, who originated from a mixture of the Ibibio and Igbo, had a different name for God. They call him *Obassi di n'elu*. By adopting the name *Chukwu* for their oracle, they wanted to convince the Igbo – and to a large extent succeeded – that they could communicate with God in Arochukwu. According to Ekejiuba:

Although Igbo groups conceived and consulted the oracle as the Supreme God (the expression *ije Chukwu* to go to the Supreme God was used to mean to consult the oracle in Arochukwu), . . . the Aro did not believe in the oracle as the Supreme God, neither did it feature in their religious and judicial system as it did in that of the rest of the Igbo.[10]

There is also proof from a long-standing custom in Igboland that the name *Chukwu* was being used for the Supreme Being from time immemorial, and probably before it was even applied to the Arochukwu oracle. The privileges and right of precedence which the Nri enjoy among most Igbo groups (including the Aro) was based on the myth mentioned earlier, which says that Eri (father of Nri) was the first man created by *Chukwu*, the High God. The Aro accept the Nri's claim of primogeniture, *Isi Ana* and consequently the myth on which it is based. This would have been unlikely if Chukwu were originally an Aro god. For it would be unthinkable for an Aro god to confer the rights of primogeniture on any person other than an Aro. This, *a priori*, proves that the name was not introduced by the missionaries.

Many examples can be quoted from, among others, the records of Reverend Taylor and other early Christian missionaries and these show that each of the names analysed above, including *Chineke*, was used by the pagans of that period to designate God. In his diary, under the date of

September 10, 1857, Reverend Taylor records this conversation with two men from Nsugbe:

'Do you know who made you and all men?' They replied, 'Tshuku'. 'What has God done for you?' 'He keeps me from everything.' 'What thing do you mean?' 'From war, and everything bad, as well as good.' 'Which thing do you call bad?' '*Amusu* (witchcraft) is a bad thing.' 'When anyone dies, where do you think he goes?' 'I think he dies and goes to Tshuku.'[11]

Also worthy of mention here is the prayer of Wammah, wife of a relation of the King of Abo, at a sacrifice which she made to her Chi in 1858. In the prayer, Wammah asks her Chi to intercede for her before God. '*Biko kpere Tshukwu abiama, gwa ya obi'm dum*', 'Beseech thee to intercede with God the spirit, tell him my heart is clean.'[12] This prayer provides not only undisputed proof that the Igbo belief in *Chukwu Abiama* predates missionary influence (the report of the prayer comes from one of the first visits of the missionaries to Abo), but also illustrates the position of the Chukwu in the Igbo world-view.

An incident reported by James Boyle, catechist in Bonny, shows that the name *Chineke* was used among the Igbo pagans of Bonny as early as 1879:

Called on Ekeke, the head priest of Bonny . . . After saluting him as he was building his house, I said, 'So you are building your house?' He replied in English, 'Yes, if God help me I will carry it through.' I interrogated, 'What? Iseneke help not Isiwu (juju)?' He said, 'No I mean Isineke (the Almighty)' . . . 'Why do you, instead of worshipping God, worship Abara?' (sic). He then said, 'God make us all and put us in Abara's care that he might look after us'.[13]

The Moslem influence

The Moslem influence in Igboland is minimal. Apart from a pocket of Moslems in Ibagwa in the Nsukka Division due to inter-marriage with the Igala, I have yet to hear of Igbo Moslems. Igbo resistance to Islam has become proverbial. Basden dedicates a complete chapter to this topic in his book published in 1921. What he said then remains true

today; 'I have made inquiries during the last seventeen
years in many directions, of missionaries, commissioners
and traders and also of intelligent natives, and have yet to
hear of the first case of an Ibo forsaking paganism for
Mohammedanism.'[14] Abandoned mosques near Umwana
in Afikpo and Orlu are evidences of failure of Islam to
infiltrate Igboland.

Many factors contribute to this Igbo resistance. Histori-
cally, Moslem conquests in West Africa never engulfed
Igboland. Islam thrives in urban areas, while most Igbos
lived in scattered homesteads. Chiefless and egalitarian,
Igbo society proved impervious to Islamic political doctrine
which favours hierarchical authoritarian structures. Different from their position in most other West African
societies, Igbo women – far from being down-trodden – are
economically and socially self-reliant and politically very
powerful. Consequently, Islam never had enough points of
contact with Igboland to make any significant impact, so
that the possibility of the Igbo concept of God being due to
contact with Moslems is very remote.

The Jewish influence

The discovery of the belief in and a high concept of God
among non-literate peoples has ever continued to intrigue
Western writers. The assumption seems to be that the concept of one God was known only among the Israelites and
this presumably was due to revelation. The paradox seems
to be, 'How can the untutored African conceive of God?' So
earlier writers on African religion made efforts to establish
the place and the route through which the idea was
exported to Africa. For West African peoples, the source of
their beliefs is invariably Israel, and the route was through
Egypt.

The celebrated work of J. J. Williams, *Hebrewisms of West
Africa*, is known to all students of West African religions. In
it, he maintains with scholarly arguments the influence of
Hebraic religion on the West African.[15] In his later book he
writes: 'Africa's concept of God is a remnant of a pure,

universal monotheism'.[16] In West Africa, he argues, this monotheistic belief was reinforced by later waves of Jewish influences. He writes: 'Somewhere in the dim past, a wave or more probably, a series of waves of Hebraic influence swept over Negro Africa, leaving unmistakable traces among the various tribes, where they have endured even to the present day'.[16]

There is not sufficient evidence to substantiate this doctrine of primitive revelation nor Jewish influence on West African beliefs. The similarity found between some West African and Jewish beliefs, is no ground to claim an identity of source or the influence of one on the other. For example, circumcision found in some West African societies, today, was known in Israel and ancient Egypt, and is still practised among Australian aborigines. If on this basis we claim an influence of Israel and Egypt on West Africa, aren't we equally justified to claim their influence on Australia or even Australian influence on Egypt?

It is more sensible to recognize the obvious fact that nature itself is one great continuous revelation of God. It is an excellent and yet mysterious work of art which continues to give us some small idea of the Almighty and Incomprehensible Artist.

The assumption that the concept of God is a preserve of Judeo-Christian culture has not even the support of the Bible, as its propounders perhaps thought. Some parts of the Bible, under the influence of Greek philosophy, not only recognized the possibility of arriving at the knowledge of God through other ways than revelation, but actually rebuked all those who have not been able to discover God. 'Yes, naturally stupid are all men who have not known God and who, from the good things that are seen, have not been able to discover Him-who-is' (Wis. 13: 1). St Paul puts it more clearly. 'Ever since God created the world, his everlasting power and deity – however invisible – have been there for the mind to see in the things he has made' (Rom. 1.20).

African traditional religion is even clearer on this. Ashanti proverbs say, 'No man's path crosses another's', i.e. 'Everyone has a direct path to God'. Again, 'No one shows a child the Supreme Being'.[17]

The Christian influence

Although the Igbo concept of God is not due to Christian contacts, a century and a quarter of interaction has had a considerable influence on a number of traditional beliefs. Paradoxically, evangelization has both obscured and clarified the Igbo concept of God. The missionaries must be given the credit for being the first to investigate and record African names and concepts of God, but it must be said that their scope for doing so was very limited. They were only concerned with finding words in the local language to translate 'God' in the Bible and in their catechisms, song books and liturgical books. This done, they condemned and rejected whatever the people knew of God as part of their superstitious pagan patrimony which Christianity had come to destroy.

Traditional Igbo praise-names and other ways of articulating their belief in God were not used in evangelization or catechetics and homilies. For example, titles of God used in Igbo prayer books and liturgical books are literal translations of Judeo-European concepts, titles like *Chineke nke igwe ndi agha*, Lord of hosts, *Chineke puru ime ihe nile*, Omnipotent God. The people were taught that God is God of Abraham, of Isaac, of Jacob, that he is the Uncaused Cause the First Cause, or, the first mover which means absolutely nothing to an African.

Their reaction to this was negative. The Igbo believed the missionaries when they said that Igbo ways of invoking and worshipping God were inferior to the Christians' ways. Consequently, they now seem to have left the worship of God to the Christians while they occupy themselves more with the worship of the lesser deities. Altars of God which used to exist in the house of every titled elder, and in some public places, are now very difficult to find. Sacrifices to God, *Ilu onu Anyanwu na Eze enu,* are now hardly ever seen, for non-Christian Igbo have identified themselves as *Ndi ogo mmuo*, 'Those who worship the spirits' as opposed to *Ndi Uka*, 'Christians who worship God'.

At the same time, by using the traditional personal names of God in the Bible and in their evangelization, the missionaries perhaps unconsciously clarified the Igbo traditional concept of God. God assumed more personal features. The God of tradition took on some of the attributes of the God of the Bible. He is now considered more accessible. He listens, hears, and grants the requests of suppliants more readily. He is now more readily associated with morality. *Chineke ekwela ihe ọjọọ*, 'May God not permit evil', is now a very common expression. The influence of Christian eschatological ideas is also evident: *Chineke kpọ gi ọkụ*, 'May God burn you', is a curse now frequently used, even by non-Christians. Perhaps the greatest influence of Christian preaching on the Igbo concept of God is that the Deity is no longer considered a power to be feared, but a loving father who is continually concerned with the welfare of his children. God is not only the father of the deities but the father of men. The deities, however, still have a very central rôle to play.

Notes

1 Smith, E. W. *African Ideas of God* (1961) p.1.
2 Parrinder, E. G. *West African Religion* (1969) p.13.
3 Correia, Alves 'L'Animisme Ibo et les Divinités de la Nigéria', *Anthropos* (1921) p.361.
4 Green, M. M. *Igbo Village Affairs* (London 1947) p.52.
5 Ezekwugo, C. U. 'Chi, The true God in Igbo Religion' Unpublished thesis, University of Innsbruck (1973) p.93.
6 Ezekwugo, C. U. ibid., p.115.
7 Crowther, S. and Taylor, J. *The Gospel on the Banks of the Niger — Niger expedition of 1857–1859* (London, 1968) p.296.
8 Equiano, Olaudah *Equiano Travels or the interesting Narrative of the life of Olaudah Equiano or Gustavus Vassa, the African* (London 1857) p.10. Equiano was born in 1745. He gave the name of his home town as Esseke, probably Isseke, now in Orlu Division.
9 Baikie, W. B. *Narrative of an Exploring Voyage up the rivers Kwora and Binue commonly known as the Niger and Tsadda* (London 1856) p.311.
10 Ekejiuba, F. 'Aro World view: An analysis of the

cosmological ideas of Arochukwu people of Eastern
Nigeria', *West African Religion*, 8 (1970) p.4.
11 Crowther, S. and Taylor, J. op. cit. (1968) p.269.
12 Crowther, S. and Taylor, J. ibid., p.348.
13 CA3/07/1-6 Niger Missions, 'Extracts from Annual
Reports' 1874–79 by J. Boyle, Native Agent, Bonny.
14 Basden, G. T. *Among the Ibos of Nigeria* (London, 1966)
p.302.
15 Williams, J. J. *Hebrewisms of West Africa* (New York,
1930) p.130.
16 Williams, J. J. *Africa's God* (Massachusetts, 1938) p.76.
17 Busia, K. A. 'The Ashanti' in *African Worlds* (1968)
p.192.

Appendix II The future of African traditional religion

African traditional religion has co-existed for centuries with other religions, notably Christianity and Islam, but its future has never been as bleak as it is today. Christianity came to north Africa in the first century A.D. and thrived for more than six centuries. Similarly, Islam was introduced into north Africa in the first century of its foundation. Within years it supplanted Christianity as the strongest religious group in the area and began to spread southwards along the east and west coasts of Africa and across the Sahara. Pockets of Coptic Christians remained in Egypt and Ethiopia. It was Islam, however, which has posed a threat to traditional religion for nearly 1,500 years, but that threat is nothing compared to the threat of complete annihilation which traditional religion encounters from the rapidly spreading Islam and Christianity in Africa today.

The spread of Islam before the last century was gradual and sometimes violent, but somehow African traditional religion managed to survive it. Sometimes it was a physical feature – the desert, the forest, or the mountain ridges which stopped the advancing Islamic forces, but in some places both religions co-existed and interacted for a long time. The West African Kingdom of Gana (further north-west of present-day Ghana) had a Moslem settlement in its capital, until it was sacked by the Ahmoravid jihadists in 1076 A.D. The other inhabitants for the most part practised traditional religion. The peaceful spread of Islam to the great empire of Mali is said to have reached its climax about 1200 A.D. The king of Jenne, thereafter known as Sultan Kunburu, assembled all the Moslems in his kingdom, over 4,000 people, and declared his acceptance of Islam before them all. Most of his subjects, however, remained in the traditional religion.[1] Islam held a great attraction for the Sudanese monarchs of this epoch because it helped them to strengthen the vital trade links with Moslem kingdoms and traders from the north. Perhaps more important, it enhanced their authority and control over the different ethnic groups which made up their vast kingdoms. Besides, Islam brought with it a superior Arabic culture with its literacy, and provided the only known contact with the civilized world. These pragmatic and utilitarian motives left the Sudanese rulers, for the most part, nominal Moslems and a vast number of their subjects still adherents of African traditional religion.

Similar situations existed in most parts of western Sudan, north of the forest belt until the Fulani reformist holy wars of the late eighteenth and early nineteenth centuries. So the period before these great jihads was a period of great interaction and interchange of ideas between Islam and the African traditional religion. The ruling classes adopted Islam, but stuck to and cherished many traditional beliefs, while the mass of the people who remained in the traditional religion adopted some Moslem habits. The jihadists wiped out the ruling class and imposed reformed Islam on the population. Groups who still resisted Islam had to emigrate southwards to take shelter in the forest zones, on the hills or in remote rural areas. However, Islam continued to spread through the traders who penetrated to the forest areas to trade in cherished commodities like dairy and cereal products and kola-nuts.

Eastern Nigeria offers a typical example of a place where the traditional religion successfully resisted Christian evangelization for nearly half a century, but has recently witnessed one of the greatest mass conversions to Christianity due to factors some of which are external to both religions. The first Christian mission outposts were set up at Calabar at the mouth of the Cross River by the Presbyterians in 1846. About a decade later, the Anglicans opened a mission at Onitsha on the east bank of the Niger. For nearly fifty years, both missions were unable to penetrate inland nor make any significant impact on the traditional society among which they had settled.[2] Similarly, the Catholic missionaries who began work at Onitsha in 1885 were limited for a long time to the towns along the river banks. The handful of converts they made were drawn from the rejects of traditional society – slaves, *Osu* or outcasts, abandoned children and so forth. There were, of course, spectacular cases of genuine conversion like Chief Idigo of Aguleri, but generally speaking, until the turn of the century, traditional religion resisted the efforts of the Christian missionaries.

Things changed, however, after 1905 when the British colonial forces occupied the area and set up a colonial régime. The missionaries came in the wake of the pacification forces and soon mission stations sprang up at the administrative centres. From these bases they began to penetrate the interior. The people wasted no time in identifying themselves with the new powers. Churches and schools were thronged, especially when it was known that a missionary could protect his adherents against the ruthless Warrant Chiefs who became agents of the new régime, and that schooling gave them immunity from forced labour. It took some time before the people were able to distinguish the missionary groups from the colonial administration, especially as both establishments were foreign and staffed by whites. Education was soon seen as a means of securing well-paid jobs. Since students who passed through any missionary school usually became adherents of the Christian denomination which ran it, different denominations vied with each other in setting up schools to 'net in' as many converts as possible.

The word 'conversion' is put in inverted commas to emphasize the fact that the embracing of Christianity by the pupils in mission schools was not always a matter of personal or free choice. Stories abound of pressures brought on pupils, and those who were reluctant to embrace Christianity were sometimes threatened with expulsion.[3] An informant told me of a case in a mission school at Onitsha in 1911 which expelled two-thirds of the pupils because they refused to give a public undertaking that they would not marry more than one wife after they left school.[4] As a pupil, I witnessed cases of parents being made to renounce traditional titles taken on behalf of their children, or face their expulsion. As waves of children became Christianized through the schools, and as young men emigrated to the urban areas in search of jobs, the structure of traditional society began to crumble and with it – traditional religion.

But the age-old traditions die hard. Very many traditional religious beliefs have persisted, even among the Christianized. For many, the change from traditional religion to Christianity was so sudden that they hardly had the time to reflect on their beliefs or to adjust to their new way of life. Consequently, many African Christians retain many traditional religious beliefs long after embracing Christianity. Innumerable instances in the pastoral field bear this out. In a certain village a few years ago, most Christians with the traditionalists went through an ordeal to clear themselves of a charge of witchcraft. When I questioned the Christians about this, one of them replied, 'I was baptized in 1910, and would never go back to any pagan practice. There is nothing evil in exposing evil men in society. We are all happy because none of our Christian members was caught by the ordeal.'[5]

The traditional African family institution which was seen as a socio-religious community of the living, the dead and those yet to be born, was the first to come under attack. Elders made desperate efforts to restrain some of their children from joining the Church schools and the Christian churches. This was for a purely religious motive, namely, if their children – because of their new religion – should fail to give them the traditional funeral rites, they themselves would not reach the spirit-land. Soon, certain families began to find among their members some Christians who refused to accept the religious authority and rôle of the Okpala, family head, as the mouthpiece of the ancestors, and would not participate in the traditional rites and rituals. The situation reached a crisis point when it fell to some Christians to act as Okpala, the bearer of the Ofo, the traditional staff of ancestral authority. Many Christians stood firm and refused to take on this rôle, which in some cases brought about a division in the family between the Christians and traditionalists. In other cases a compromise was reached, which permitted the Christian to fulfil the social functions while a traditionalist kept the Ofo and fulfilled the religious rôle. In many cases, however, some Christians slid back into the traditional religion.

The same sort of problem faced the village-head or the chief at the political level. The position of the chief as the *Okpala* and religious leader of the village-group was seriously challenged and sometimes undermined. His power, already reduced by colonial rule, was greatly threatened by the comparatively wealthy and educated élite who took over power from the colonial masters. Christians refused to accept the religious rôle of the chief and his claim to be the mouthpiece of the ancestors. For some time, his office appeared irrelevant. However, interest in the institution of chieftaincy revived when the government decided to set up a House of Chiefs in the then Eastern Region. Even communities which had never had chieftaincy institutions began to create and install chiefs. To prove their authenticity, they went through the traditional religious rites of installation. Areas which had traditionally had chiefs revived their traditional religious rôles. About Onitsha which possesses a long-respected chieftaincy tradition, Meek wrote, 'The people of Onitsha have adopted Christianity in no uncertain manner, and the Obi himself has become a Roman Catholic. All that remains to him of his old prestige is the presidency of a society which functions feebly, and a certain sentimental regard by the people'.[6]

Since Meek wrote this, things have changed. The last two Obi of Onitsha have been non-practising Christians and faithfully performed their traditional religious rôles.

Many traditionally cherished ideals of family life have come into conflict with Christian practices. Most controversial were the various forms of traditional marriage, especially the question of the dowry and polygamy. Most churches never really condemned the traditional processes of contracting marriages, including the dowry. However, they recognized it as no more than a betrothal rite for Christians, who still have to go through a church wedding as in Europe. In recent years, many Nigerians have begun to ask why a Church minister could not witness and bless the marriage during the traditional ceremonies, especially in view of the fact that the Church has insisted all along on the exclusion of traditional religious rites. This would certainly avoid an unnecessary duplication which involves the couples in so much expense and trouble. Many couples live together until they save enough money to go through the Church wedding.

On the other hand, the Church has condemned several forms of marriage recognized by traditional religion. These include various legalized forms of concubinage and polygamy. The stand of the Church has been consistent and uncompromising. Polygamous converts have been denied baptism. Africans, who traditionally value large families as status symbols and signs of divine blessing, have never come to terms with the Church's stand on polygamy. Many Christians have compromised by lapsing into polygamy after receiving the major sacraments – Baptism, Eucharist, Confirmation and Marriage, *Ozo ndi uka* – 'Christian titles', as they are called. The more sophisticated city dwellers prefer to house several wives in different flats to safeguard their prestige and avoid the inconveniences of running a polygamous home in urban circumstances. A bold move by the Roman Catholic Church to tighten control by denying polygamist Christians public burial nearly led to a schism. The polygamists reacted sharply by threatening to form a St David's Church. David, a servant of God in the Old Testament, they argued, had several wives. The Church eventually backed down, and allowed Christian funeral rites for polygamists.

In other areas traditional religion lost heavily because of the process of social change brought about by western education and industrialization. As the young people became educated and left for the cities, many traditional rituals involving the young people fell into disuse. When jobs backed by school-leaving certificates brought in more money, it became fashionable to go to school and become a Christian. Traditionalists rushed to have their children baptized in the belief that that would put them on the path to prosperity. Christianity in time became associated with the modern way of life which meant adopting European names, some education, European clothes, paid jobs, enlightenment and prosperity. With time, most of the shrines of the deities began to crumble, traditional feasts were neglected and associations which brought the young and the old together became obsolete. Traditional religion thus is fast becoming the preserve of an aging minority who live in the countryside.

Among the many traditional institutions which have resisted the sweeping changes brought about by Christianity, institutions which meet crisis situations feature prominently. This may be because Christianity has not succeeded in finding substitutes for them. Such institutions as traditional funeral rites, the rôle of Ala as custodian of law and order in village life, ordeals, rituals to avert misfortunes, diviners and medicine-men have continued to thrive and are used by both traditionalists and Christians alike. The Igbo, and I believe most Africans, have never accepted the dull, gloomy, mournful Christian funeral service. This is very opposed to their idea of death as 'going home' and funeral rites as a worthy tribute to one who has led a successful life. Much drumming and dancing, salutes, display of acts of bravery, and wealth feature prominently to demonstrate the passing-away of a powerful and prosperous man, and to announce his arrival to take his place among the notables in the spirit-world.

A quiet funeral is described as ọnwụ ọkụkọ, death of a fowl. Many prosperous Christians would wish for traditional funerals for themselves and their relatives, and sometimes do involve themselves in traditional rites which their religion condemns. Even today, many Christians as well as pagans appeal to Ala and/or other deities for the protection of their property. People insist on swearing on the shrines of the local spirits because it is more effective. 'The Bible does not kill', they say. Traditional ordeals are frequently used to detect criminals, sorcerers and witches. Divination, fortune-telling and medicine-making services have grown into large businesses far beyond the limits of their traditional religious rôles. They now flourish in the supposedly more Christianized urban areas, where the pressures of modern life create more crisis situations.

And yet Christianity has had a profound influence on traditional religion. It has certainly made the traditional concept of God clearer to the African. God is now seen to be more personal, loving and approachable. The idea of God as a rewarder of the good and punisher of the wicked is now accepted, but not the Christian ideas of heaven and hell.

Much of the fear and many of the taboos which characterized traditional religion have disappeared because
Christians have broken them all and not died, as it was
traditionally believed they would. But on the whole, Christianity has had a negative influence on the traditional structures on which traditional religion was based, throwing
them into disarray. Being a religion which required more
communal rather than individual worship-responses, once
the factors which united the groups were weakened, it
began to crumble.

Most traditionalists do not practise any religion today
because they cannot, since the family, their contemporaries
and the elders are now scattered. The traditional direct
sacrifices to God and his altars are now difficult to find
because they require the feasting of members of one age-
group and in many areas they are the ones who have joined
the new religion. It is also true that the worship of God has
deteriorated because the traditionalists have tended to
identify themselves as *ndi ọgọ mmụọ*, 'those who worship the
deities', in contrast to the Christians, who worship God. The
religious indifference and secularism rife in Christian cir-
cles have both begun to affect traditional religion. It is now
very common to hear sceptical remarks from traditionalists
such as *uka di n'obi*, 'Religion is in the heart'; 'every object of
religious belief is manmade', 'whatever you believe in works
for you'. Or, as the remarks made by the Islanders of Lake
Victoria, 'My fire is my God, for it cooks the food I eat.'[7]

The threat posed by Christianity and Islam has made
some adherents of traditional religion reflect on their
belief. Many have joined one of the two world religions,
many others have moved farther away from the traditional
religion by neglecting some of its monotheistic practices,
others have lapsed into scepticism and have become
publicly indifferent, which was once unthinkable. One
would have expected that after almost a century of contact
with Christianity and a millennium with Islam, traditional
religion would have adopted the powerful organizational
systems and book-based apostolate used by the two world
religions. As long as it does not reform itself sufficiently to
meet modern needs and developments it will continue to be

a dwindling minority, and its total extinction will only be a matter of time.

Notes

1 Parrinder, G. E. *Religion in Africa* (1969) p.180.
2 Ogbu Kalu (ed.) *Christianity In West Africa: The Nigerian Story* (1977) p.308.
3 Isichei, E. 'Ibo and Christian Beliefs, Some Aspects of a Theological Encounter', *African Affairs*, vol. 68 (1969) p.124.
4 Interview with Chief R. R. Olisa, the Atamanya of Osomari (June 1974).
5 Interview with members of the Local Church Council (LCC) of Nkwelle-Awka Village, St. Patrick's Parish (May 1972).
6 Meek, C. K. *Law and Authority in a Nigerian Tribe* (1937) p.195.
7 Taylor, J. V. *The Primal Vision* (1969) p.82.

Bibliography

African Arts (magazine published by African Studies Center, University of California).

Alutu, J. O. *A Groundwork of Nnewi History* (E.N.I.S. Press, Enugu, 1963).

Anozia, I. P. 'The Religious Import of Igbo Names', unpublished thesis, Urban University, Rome (1968).

Arinze, F. A. *Sacrifice in Ibo Religion* (Ibadan University Press, 1970).

Baikie, W. B. *Narrative of an Exploring Voyage up the Rivers Kwora and Binue, commonly known as the Niger and Tsadda, in 1854* (London, 1856).

Bascom, W. *Ifa Divination: Communication Between Gods and Men in West Africa* (Indiana University Press, London, 1969).

Basden, G. T. *Niger Ibos* (repr. Frank Cass, London, 1966).

Basden, G. T. *Among the Ibos of Southern Nigeria* (repr. Frank Cass, London, 1966).

Busia, K. A. 'The Ashanti' in *African Worlds*, ed. Forde, Daryll (1968).

Correia, P. I. A. 'Le Sens Moral chez les Ibos de la Nigéria', in *Anthropos*, 18–19 (1923–1924) pp.880–889.

Correia, P. I. A. 'L'Animisme Ibo et les Divinités de la Nigéria', *Anthropos*, 16–17 (1921–1922) pp.360–366.

Crowther, S. and Taylor, J. *The Gospel on the Banks of the Niger, Niger Expedition, 1857 to 1859* (repr. London, 1968).

Damman, E. 'A Tentative Philological Typology of some African High Deities' *Journal of Religion in Africa*, II (1970) p.6.

Danquah, J. B. *The Akan Doctrine of God* (London, 1944).

Downes, R. M. *Tiv Religion* (Ibadan University Press, 1971).

Driberg, J. H. 'The Secular Aspects of Ancestor Worship in Africa', Supplement to the *Journal of Royal African Society*, Vol. 35 (Jan. 1936).

Ekanem, I. *The 1963 Nigerian Census, A Critical Appraisal* (Benin City, Ethiope Publishing Corporation 1972).

Ekejiuba, F. 'Aro World View' in *West African Religion* (Journal of Religious Studies Dept., Nsukka University of Nigeria) (1970).

Equiano, Olaudah *Equiano Travels; The Interesting Narrative of the life of Olaudah Equiano or Gustavus Vassa, the African*, London (1867).

Evans-Pritchard, E. E. *Nuer Religion* (Oxford, 1970).

Ezeanya, S. N. in *Biblical Revelation and African Beliefs*, ed. Dickson, Kwesi A. and Ellingworth, Paul (New York, 1969).

Ezekwugo, C. 'Chi, The True God in Igbo Religion', unpublished thesis, Innsbruck University (1973).

Field, M. J. *Search for Security* (London, 1960).

Forde, Daryll (ed.) *African Worlds* (Oxford University Press, London, 1968).

Forde, Daryll and Jones, G. I. *The Ibo and Ibibio-Speaking Peoples of South-eastern Nigeria* (International African Institute, London, 1962).

Green, M. M. *Igbo Village Affairs* (London, 1947).

Griaule, Marcel *Conversations with Ogotemmeli* (Oxford University Press, London, 1965).

Horton, W. R. C. 'God, Man, and Land in a Northern Ibo Village-Group', *Africa*, 26 (Jan. 1956) pp.17–28.

Idowu, B. *Olodumare, God in Yoruba Belief* (Longmans, London, 1962).

Ilogu, E. 'Ofo: A Religious and Political Symbol', *Nigerian Magazine* (Sept. 1964) p.234.

Isichei, E. 'Ibo and Christian Beliefs, Some Aspects of a Theological Encounter', *African Affairs*, Vol. 68 (1969) p.124.

Jeffreys, M. D. W. 'The Umundri Traditions of Origin', *African Studies*, 15 (3 Sept. 1956) pp.119–131.

Jeffreys, M. D. W. 'Ikenga – The ram-headed God' *African Studies*, Vol. 13, 1 (1965) p.40.

Jordan, J. P. *Bishop Shanahan of Southern Nigeria* (Dublin, 1971 ed.).

Leonard, A. G. The *Lower Niger and Its Tribes* (London, 1968 ed.).

Le Roy, Mgr. *Les Religions des Primitifs* (Paris, 1906).

Lévy-Bruhl, L. *Les Fonctions Mentales dans les Sociétés Inférieures* (2nd ed., 1912).

Malinowski, B. 'Myths in Primitive Society' in *Magic, Science and Religion* (1954) p.107.

Marcuse, Herbert *One Dimensional Man* (Abacus ed., London, 1972).

Mbiti, J. S. *African Religions and Philosophy* (Heinemann, London, 1971).

Mbiti, J. S. *Concepts of God in Africa* (London, 1970).

Meek, C. K. *Law and Authority in a Nigerian Tribe* (London, 1937).

Metuh, Emefie 'The Supreme God in Igbo Life and Worship', *Journal of Religion in Africa*, Vol. V.

Noon, A. John 'A Preliminary Examination of Death Concept of the Ibo', *American Anthropologist*, No. 44 (1944) p.640.

Nwokocha, C. A. 'The Kola: Igbo Symbol of Love and Unity', unpublished thesis, Urban University, Rome (1969).

Obi, C. 'Igbo Marriage and Christianity', unpublished thesis, Urban University, Rome (1970).

Obiefuna, A. 'The Christian Education of Igbo Moral Conscience', unpublished thesis, Rome (1966).

O'Connell, J. 'The withdrawal of the High God in West African Religion: An Essay of interpretation', *Man*, 42, Article 109 (1962) pp.67–69.

Ottenberg, S. 'Ibo Receptivity to Change' in *Continuity and Change in African Cultures*, ed. Bascom, W. B. and Herskovits, J. M. (Chicago, 1958).

Parrinder, G. E. *West African Religion* (Epworth Press ed., London, 1969).

Parrinder, G. E. *Religion in Africa* (Penguin ed., Harmondsworth, 1969).

Parrinder, G. E. *African Traditional Religion* (Hutchinson, London, 1954).

Shelton, A. J. 'On the Recent Interpretation of Deus

Otiosus, the Withdrawal of High God in West African
Religion', *Man*, 64 (1964), p.53.

Shelton, A. J. 'The Presence of the Withdrawn High God
in North Ibo Religious Belief and Worship', *Man*, 65,
No. 4 (1965) p.15.

Smith, E. W. (ed.) *African Ideas of God* (Edinburgh House
Press, London, 1961).

Talbot, P. A. *Some Nigerian Fertility Cults* (repr. Frank
Cass, London, 1967).

Talbot, P. A. *The Peoples of Southern Nigeria* (London,
1926) 4 vols.

Talbot, P. A. *The Tribes of the Niger Delta* (London, 1932).

Taylor, J. V. *The Primal Vision* (SCM Press London, 1969).

Tempels, P. *Bantu Philosophy* (Présence Africaine ed.,
Paris, 1969).

Thomas, Northcote *Anthropological Report on the Ibo
Speaking Peoples of Nigeria* (London, 1914) Vols I-IV.

Turner, V. W. 'Myth and Symbol' in *International
Encyclopedia of the Social Sciences*, Vol. 10 (1969).

Uchendu, V. C. *The Igbo of Southeast Nigeria* (Holt,
Rinehart and Winston, New York, 1965).

Westermann, D. *Africa and Christianity* (Oxford University
Press, 1937).

Wieschoff, W. A. 'Social Significance of Names among
the Ibos of Nigeria', in *American Anthropologist*, 43 (1941)
p.212.

Williams, J. J. *Hebrewisms of West Africa* (New York, 1930).

Williams, J. J. *Africa's God* (Massachusetts, 1938).

Wilson, Monica *Religion and the Transformation of Society*
(1971).

Unpublished documents

Manuscripts of the Niger Mission in C.M.S. Archives London

These documents have now been moved to the University
Library, Birmingham, England.

CA3/04/529 Niger Missions, 'Journal, Reports and
Correspondences' of Solomon Perry, Native Agent,
Onitsha, 1879–1880.

CA3/04/747A-C   Niger Missions, 'Review of the Niger Mission' by Rev. Solomon Perry, Native Agent, Onitsha, 1878.

CA3/04/528   Niger Missions, 'Correspondence' of James Boyle, Native Agent with Bishop S. A. Crowther, Onitsha, 1879–80.

CA3/07/1–6   Niger Missions, 'Extracts from Annual Reports' 1874–79 by James Boyle, Native Agent, Bonny.

CA3/09/1–10   Niger Missions, 'Letters' (1878–1880), 'Annual Reports and Journal Extracts' by Rev. John Buck, Native Pastor (1871–1875 Onitsha, 1876-1880 Alenso).

CA3/013/20   Niger Missions, 'Gabon Conference Paper on Polygamy' by Mr. Fuller.

CA3/015/1   Niger Missions, 'Journal Extracts' of J. During, Catechist, Native Agent, Osomare, 1878.

CA3/020/1–4   Niger Missions, 'Reports' of John Thomas, Native School Master, Onitsha, 1865–69.

CA3/022/1–2   Niger Missions, 'Journal Extracts' of John W. Fortunatus, Native Catechist, Brass, 1874, 1879.

CA3/025/1–4   Niger Missions, 'Journal Extracts' 1866–1867, 'Annual Letters' (1862, 1872) by Rev. Francis Langley, Native Pastor, Onitsha.

CA3/029/1–4   Niger Missions, 'Journals' of Rev. Daniel Peeler, Native School Master, Osomare, 1878–1879.

CA3/030/1–11   Niger Missions, 'Reports' of Rev. Solomon S. Perry, Native Pastor, Onitsha, 1872–1880.

CA3/034/1–9   Niger Missions, 'Quarterly Journal Extracts' by William Romaine, Native Pastor, Onitsha, 1859–1872.

CA3/035/7   Niger Missions, 'Journal Excerpts' by W. Smart, Native Pastor, Bonny, 1868–76.

CA3/036/1   Niger Missions, 'Journal' by John Smart, Native Catechist, Onitsha, 1858–59.

CA3/037/57   Niger Missions, 'A Report on the political and spiritual state of Onitsha' (1864) No. 36, by Rev. John Christopher Taylor, Native Pastor, Onitsha.

CA3/041/1–4   Niger Mission, 'Journals, Annual Reports' by John Williams, Native Schoolmaster, Onitsha, 1875–1879.

Interviews and other manuscripts

Achu, A. T. 'Life after death in Igbo Religion',
    Unpublished dissertation, Project MS. T.I.M.E., Lagos
    (1975).
Arazu 'The Pagan', unpublished MS. A tape-recorded
    interview of an Igbo elder called Ezenwadeyi.
Interview of Dr. Arazu by Emefie Ikenga Metuh.
Onwuejeogwu, M. A. 'An Ethno-Historical Survey of
    Igbo West and East of the Lower Niger', unpublished
    MS (1969).
Tape-recorded interview of Nweke Ezeamalu, of Awba,
    Awka Division, Jan. 1972.
Tape-recorded interview of some elders at Ebenebe, Awka
    Division.
Tape-recorded interview of Enukora Nwosu, head-priest
    of Amikwo, Awka.
Igba afa n'ani Igbo, a Programme on Radio Nigeria, Enugu,
    13th April, 1972.
Tape-recorded interview of Ezenwako the Ezeana of
    Umudioka, Awka, 4th May, 1974.
Tape-recorded interview of Ikwue Anikwue, elder of
    Amanuke, Awka Division, June 1972.
Tape-recorded interview of Ubanwaogaranya
    Chukwukezie, elder of Okija, Ihala Division, July 1974.
Tape-recorded interview of Ukpabi Ulasi of Otolo, Nnewi,
    July 1974.
Tape-recorded interview of Nwafor Okafor, an Aro elder
    resident at Nnewi, July 1974.
Tape-recorded interview of Chief A. E. Metuh, elder of
    Otolo-Nnewi, Aug. 1974.
Tape-recorded interview of Okafor Awili, Otolo-Nnewi,
    Sept. 1975.
Tape-recorded interview of Amos Chukwukelu, elder of
    Okija, July 1974.
Tape-recorded interview of Chief Oduah of Ogwu Ikpele,
    Ogbaru Division, July 1974.
Interview of Chief R. R. Olisa, the Atamamya of Osomari,
    June 1974.
Interview with members of the Local Church Council
    (LCC) of Nkwelle-Awka Village, St. Patrick's Parish,
    May 1972.